Diary of
Military Government in
Germany
1945

Portrait, in oils, of the Author, June 1945.
By Gregor Sajcowicz

Diary of
Military Government in
Germany
1945

B. N. Reckitt

ARTHUR H. STOCKWELL LTD.
Elms Court   Ilfracombe
Devon

By the same author:
  Charles I and Hull
  The History of Reckitt & Sons Ltd.
  The Lindley Affair
  A History of the Sir James Reckitt Charity
  A History of the Albert Reckitt Charitable Trust
  A History of the Sir Philip Reckitt Educational Trust

ISBN 0 7223 2301-8
Printed in Great Britain by
Arthur H. Stockwell Ltd.
Elms Court   Ilfracombe
Devon

CONTENTS

LIST OF ILLUSTRATIONS

"Military Government exists to keep the civil population from under the feet of the Army."

Eisenhower

FOREWORD

This Diary was written up from notes, made daily at the time, shortly after my demobilisation in August 1945. It therefore reflects events as experienced, without any modifications which might have been made in the light of subsequent history. Relations with other groups whether British, American, Russian or German, have not been disguised in any way and I apologise for any remarks which might give offence pleading only that they are what I thought at the time.

    My thanks are due to my stepdaughter, Sarah Bradley, for faultless typing.

B.N.R.

Diary of
Military Government
in Germany

Preliminaries

First an application to join Civil Affairs was sent in from Northern Ireland early in 1944, when the future of Anti-Aircraft Artillery looked unpromising. The air raids were over and there was no chance of action in that 'back-door' area. This was followed by an interview with a War Office board in London when Anti-Aircraft Command was very much alive again in the fight against the V1 and my regiment was in action around Hythe; and finally there came an order to attend a six-week course at the Civil Affairs Staff School at Wimbledon. This was early in September 1944 when the V1 battle was over and there was nothing left for Anti-Aircraft to do but tidy up the innumerable sites it had occupied on the south coast between Eastbourne and Dover.

The Wimbledon course was the first to deal with Germany alone, Civil Affairs' detachments being already deployed in France and Belgium. The Hun was practically back on his own frontiers and it was expected that he would capitulate at any moment. The atmosphere at the school was therefore one of urgency and haste. The teaching was based on preliminary 'behind the line' work and on subsequently taking over a country which, though it had surrendered, was otherwise an uninvaded going concern. It was assumed that its officials and administration would be in being, though perhaps creaking badly at the joints as the results of five years of war and heavy bombing of industries and communications. This assumption, which was to turn out so wrong, was at the root of the failure of much of the planning for Germany. In too many cases the action which we were taught to take presupposed the existence of communications and transport which, when it came to actual practice, just did not exist. As an instance, the transport which in theory we should have used to evacuate displaced persons was much more urgently needed for

13

army use, and we never did have any communications with the formations for which we were supposed to be working until long after the war was over. But apart from this the course gave indispensable basic instruction on German history, civil administration, economics, law, food supply and a host of other subjects. It also covered military staff duties, both British and American, which in the latter case turned out hardly necessary. The Americans did not apply staff procedure to British Military Government detachments under their command. We often wished that they would since an occasional written order is helpful.

The most useful practicable piece of wisdom which I took away with me from Wimbledon was the answer to a question as to what was the first thing to do on taking over a town in ruins, lacking food, electricity and water supplies, threatened with an epidemic and overrun with rioting displaced persons . . . . The answer was form a police force, for without some semblance of law and order none of the problems could be tackled.

At the end of the course some unlucky ones had disappeared, a few received promotion and the bulk retained their ranks as staff officers, grades I and II. We had acquired a vast mass of undigested information in the form of notes, but found later that we had perhaps learned more than we thought at the time.

There was much debate at the school as to how the Germans were to be treated — the extremists favouring outright brutality, but the majority something between fairness and harshness. The more violent gentlemen were very little different from the others when it came to practice.

From Wimbledon we went to the Civil Affairs mobilisation and training centre at the Grand Hotel, Eastbourne, where we did very little training and for months no mobilisation. Theoretically we were there from October 1944 to April 1st 1945, but in practice most of us were able to be away from the place on leave and duty during most of that time, and when we were there we were busy planning how to get away. Not that the Grand Hotel was uncomfortable — rather the reverse — but the routine was irritating and boredom resulted. The only drawback to the hotel was the absence of any latches or locks on the bedroom doors. In a wind they banged all night. They had been removed at the insistance of some over-zealous 'fire precautions' officer in the interest of safety from fire. We had German language classes morning and evening and 'functional' training for the rest of the day, varied by ineffectual exercises.

My function was Trade and Industry and we soon decided that

the best form of 'functional' training consisted in visits to British industry, of which we knew little apart from our own particular peace-time activities. And it turned out that we were right, though our frequent absences were regarded as something of a 'racket'.

We visited the Pirelli Cable Works at Southampton, a foundry and cement works at Lewes, the Battersea Power Station, a tannery, clothing factory, silk printing works, paper making plant and polish factory in the London area. Then, further afield, English Electric at Rugby, the big steelworks at Hadfields and Steel, Peach and Toyer at Sheffield, the ICI plant at Billingham and their dye-stuffs works at Manchester and Huddersfield. Everywhere we were treated with great hospitality and we ate many a good boardroom luncheon.

This industrial tour was cut short in my case by being posted to attend a six-week staff duties course at Camberley on 23rd February. Civil Affairs officers had been found in practice to be profoundly ignorant of military procedure. This might have been foreseen had it been realised that very few had ever been staff officers. So it was decreed that as many as possible should do the six-month Camberley course in a potted six-week version.

It was a very hard course indeed. Most of the officers were back from Holland, Belgium and France and had practical Civil Affairs experience, but knowledge of army procedure varied from some staff experience to none: and mostly it was none. This made teaching difficult and it was made more difficult by the constant disappearance of officers as the spring offensive grew and they were recalled to their detachments. I was one of the last to go and left for Eastbourne with Major Morrish on March 27th, ten days before the course was due to end, but just in time to avoid an all-night training exercise.

The Rhine had been crossed by 21 Army Group on the 23rd March.

At Eastbourne half our Civil Affairs group (Number 9) had already crossed the channel, and all was confusion amongst the other half as they collected and tried to organise transport and sort themselves into detachments. I asked for and was reluctantly granted two days' leave, and was back by 29th March. I found myself in command of the 'increment' — that is all those specialist officers (about half the total) — who were not formed into regular detachments and who were supposed to be allotted when the time came and as the need for their technical knowledge arose.

Colonel Armitage, whom I had known in Northern Ireland, was in command of the half-group and there were several other full colonels whose jobs were undetermined. Some of them in fact were given no appointments for months after crossing the channel.

When I first entered the officers' mess at the Grand Hotel, Eastbourne, I heard, amidst the babel of voices, a high-pitched one outstripping all the others. This turned out to be that of Colonel D. A. 'Pip' Stirling, a regular ex-lancer soldier who had served in the cavalry in many theatres of war. I was at first alarmed by that voice, but, as his second-in-command throughout my service in Germany, I learned to respect his firm yet humorous character, his kindliness and unorthodox treatment of the military machine.

The group was fully lorry-borne and carried large quantities of stores which turned out not to be necessary; such as anti-gas equipment and a camera for photographing ancient monuments. All this later had to be dumped.

Most of the officers and other ranks had met for the first time within the last week or so, and they were in about equal numbers. One movement exercise had been held and the drivers were reasonably good. But many of the clerks could barely spell and many senior NCOs were with us only because no one else would have them. Our RSM (Kenward) of the RAC was excellent and gave invaluable help.

Such was the somewhat motley crowd which waited to move off on March 31st. The date of departure was a very open secret.

Military Government Detachments

In theory a Military Government group was to take over an area of about *regierungsbezirke** size, and was organised in halves; one half consisted of the commander and specialist officers and the other of detachments of four officers each, to which were to be allocated the towns in the area. In Military Government jargon the detachments were called 'bricks' because they could be added to each other if the size of a town warranted more than one detachment. In practice when this was tried it proved unworkable because two commanders were involved and questions of seniority at once arose. These were difficult to solve with officers from the British Army, RAF and Canadian Army involved, but it was generally preferable for the commander of the original detachment to have ultimate authority over both detachments because of his greater knowledge of the place and the fact that the Germans already looked to him for orders. In practice it was much better to add officers, if necessary, to the detachment and this was usually done. Many of the specialist officers were sent out from headquarters permanently, to places such as Dortmund, both to increase the local strength and because they could do their work much better on the spot.

The basic detachment was supposed to consist of a commander (who might be a lieutenant-colonel or major), a public safety officer (generally a policeman in khaki) and two others, one of whom should be trained in the handling of displaced persons. Actually detachments were made up from any material available and each officer had had specialist training of some kind which he had to subordinate to the needs of the moment.

* Roughly corresponding to an English county

B

April 1st 1945 (Easter Sunday)   Eastbourne to Tilbury   Sunday

We left in convoy early in the morning and were met near Orpington by London police guides on motor cycles who took us through the City without a stop and regardless of traffic-lights. One incident was interesting. We were halted opposite a row of workmen's houses where many convoys must have halted before. The men, who were thirsty, asked for drinks and were freely given tea, bottles of beer and minerals by still enthusiastic housewives. At the staging camp near Grays all but the drivers and myself debussed and went to fairly comfortable quarters. I took the fifty-six vehicles on to the car-park and spent a miserable night of wind and rain in a tent by the side of an arterial road. The drivers' mess was beneath a bridge carrying the road and was consequently somewhat draughty. It seemed primitive for a camp through which a large part of the Liberation Army had passed earlier in the year. But the staging camp at Southampton was very much worse, if that was any consolation.

April 2nd   Embarkation   Monday

Reveille was at 4 a.m., and the vehicles went straight down to Tilbury Docks to be loaded onto an L.S.T. (landing ship tanks). They were driven on board through the bows which opened in two doors outward and let down a ramp. Half were raised by hydraulic lifts to the upper deck and lashed down. Quarters, except for a few lucky senior officers in the ship's officers' cabins, were poor and crowded. A strong gale was blowing in the channel and the prospect of a comfortable crossing was poor. We recalled tales of the previous Civil Affairs group to cross, whose vessel had lain off the Arromanches Mulberry port for a week with only twenty-four hours' rations on board, because of bad weather.

We sailed down the Thames in the evening with two other crowded L.S.T.s, and lay off Southend for the night awaiting an escort.

April 3rd   Disembarkation at Ostend   Tuesday

Next morning the gale had died away and we made a very pleasant, sunny crossing to Ostend. Enemy submarines were reported to be about and our destroyer screen was busy with depth charges, but there were no other signs of war. The course was buoyed throughout to mark the swept channel. Dunkirk, which was then still occupied by 'forlorn hope' Germans, appeared quiet.

Disembarkation at Ostend was complicated. Our convoy organisation depended on vehicles following each other in order,

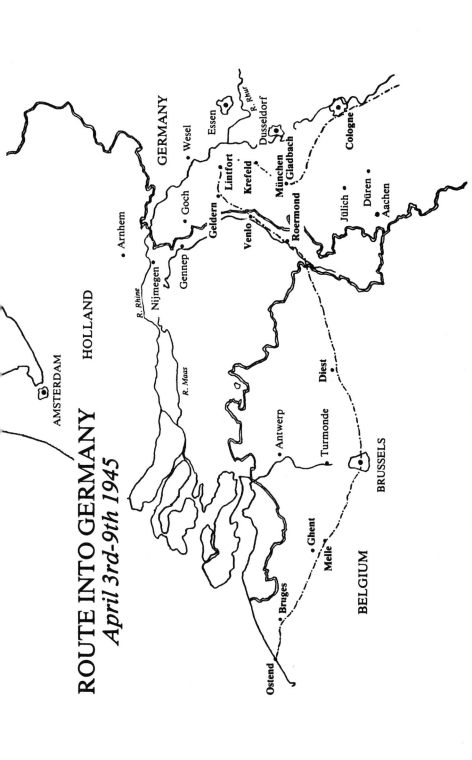

ROUTE INTO GERMANY
April 3rd–9th 1945

each being marked with large chalk figures to give its correct place. They drove off the boat out of order and there was no room on the docks to re-sort them. After some futile efforts — rendered hopeless by incoming traffic — we went on hoping that no lorries were missing.

We spent the night in a Belgian barracks recently vacated by the Germans and in good condition. There we found orders awaiting us.

Colonel D. A. Stirling was to take over command from Colonel Armitage, and the latter and the other full colonels were to leave us for separate destinations. We were to move to Lintfort in Germany and come under command of the US Ninth Army. Our area in Germany looked likely to be overrun by that army, though it would ultimately be part of the British zone of occupation. Moreover the Americans were lamentably short of Military Government staff. To prevent difficulties in serving with our allies, US officers were to be appointed technically in command of the half-group and its detachments, but actually to serve as liaison officers — a scheme which only partly matured and was not a happy one.

Maps were issued and it was decided to move to Lintfort in two stages, staying a night at Diest in Belgium.

The Ostend dock area was badly smashed but the town itself was practically untouched and full of troops. We visited a crowded but good officers' club and said farewell to our late commander.

April 5th   **Diest to Lintfort**   **Thursday**

We entered the area of recent fighting and passed not very far south of Nijmegen and Arnhem. All along the sides of the road were burnt out German cars, lorries and tanks and a very few Allied vehicles. The roads became worse and there were long waits while convoys crossed light Bailey bridges, one by one. The traffic was very heavy, nearly all moving 'up'. Frequently we would get behind another, slower convoy and I would have to decide whether I would pass it and risk my lorries becoming dovetailed into it and so possibly led the wrong way, or follow at a slower pace until it stopped for a rest. No turning was possible, so map reading had to be impeccable. Any vehicle breaking down was promptly overturned off the road so as not to impede traffic.

We crossed the Dutch border and entered Venlo. That place was represented by heaps of bricks on either side of the road and nothing else. Then came the Maas bridge, a pontoon very well made by US engineers, at Geldern. That place was also completely wrecked. We were in Germany at 1530 hours, and I addressed the troops on what it means to be in an enemy country; touching lightly on the question of non-fraternisation. Officers solemnly loaded their revolvers. Automatically we became a group of Military Government instead of Civil Affairs; a much sterner body.

It rained continuously and the mud on the roads — where they swung away across country to a temporary bridge — was deep and difficult. Sometimes for miles it had been pushed aside by bulldozers to form a continuous wall along the sides of the road.

Soon after crossing the Maas we were met by a British guide and led down atrocious byways to Lintfort. This is a small German mining town and was undamaged. We were billeted in a sort of 'garden village' consisting of comfortable middle-class houses. The owners had been turned out or had fled leaving all their possessions, but either German refugees or US troops had been looting. Every wardrobe and cupboard had been turned out and its contents scattered on the floor. Even the children's toys were smashed and strewn around. Soldiers had slept in the beds in their boots and left the filthy remains of their meals in the kitchens. There were holes in the ceilings through which shots had been fired into the rooms above to discourage snipers, and there was little or no glass in the windows.

In my house a big clock still ticked and chimed dismally every quarter through the night.

April 6th   **Lintfort**   **Friday**

The weather was better and we settled down to improving our billets and cleaning and washing clothing (the latter a most tedious job).

The US Ninth Army headquarters had moved on and Colonel Stirling was busy trying to find out what we were to do next. At last he came back with orders. The area we were to occupy, South Westphalia, would partly be captured by the US First Army from the south. Detachments which were to go to places in the north (and that meant most of them since the north included much of the Ruhr industrial area), were therefore to join the Ninth Army by a detour to the north, and take over such places as were thought fit until their final towns were taken. They were to leave the next day and we were to see no more of them for some weeks to come.

Two detachments (destined for the south) together with the commander and 'increment' were to make a detour to the south and join the First Army, but this party was to leave later.

The agreement between US and British staffs was that we were to be put into our proper places as soon as possible and that the 'increment' was not to be dispersed. The Ninth Army kept to the bargain, but the First ignored it completely and as a result the 'increment' obtained much valuable, unintended experience. Most functions such as legal, finance and my own could not, in any case,

SKETCH MAP
To show position 6th April 1945

start work until some semblance of civil organisation was in being.

April 7th   **Lintfort**   **Saturday**
All except the 'increment' and two detachments left us and we made
ourselves more comfortable by concentrating on the best houses. I
had a bath.

The two remaining detachments were to form the Rb detachment
or the nucleus of the Military Government headquarters for the
regierungsbezirk (or county) at Arnsberg, to which the functional
officers would be attached; and by Major Swayne — who was to
take over the local area or *kreis* of Arnsberg. We also had another
detachment not belonging to our group, attached to us.

Our US liaison officer, joined us from the Riviera where he had
passed a very pleasant winter. He carried a letter to say that he was
to command us, but this was difficult as Colonel Stirling was senior
in rank. It was agreed that his main job was liaison with US forces.

April 8th   **Lintfort**   **Sunday**
US Ninth Army considerately sent us their Military Government
experts to discuss procedure. We were not much the wiser as
specialist work had not yet started and they could only quote the
textbooks which we had already read. But they told us about
'casums' — daily reports on every conceivable subject which had to
be sent in to the formation to which one was attached. We did very
little of that until we reached Arnsberg as we seldom knew where
our formation was and in any case had no means of
communication with it.

April 9th   **Lintfort to Bad Godesberg**   **Monday**
We travelled south through devastated towns and villages. Krefeld
was just another heap of ruins. Outside Cologne we were turned back
by military police and made to bypass it, but we caught a glimpse of
the spires of the cathedral standing up through the haze.

At the beginning of the *autobahn*, a great double-tracked motor
road running south from Cologne, we halted to await news from
Colonel Stirling who had gone ahead to find the headquarters of
the First Army. We made a meal of our K-rations — American
emergency packs including everything from chewing-gum to
chocolate. They were good and full of vitamins, but presupposed
hot water and became somewhat tedious after a day or two.

A dispatch-rider arrived and told us to travel on to Bonn. There
Colonel Stirling met us and told us that he had failed to find the
army headquarters but had arranged billets for the night at Bad
Godesberg. The First Army appeared to have moved on to

Marburg and we should have to follow the next day if we were to catch up with the war.

Bad Godesberg was practically undamaged and we were billeted in a dirty hotel staffed by Russian girls who appeared to do little cleaning, whatever else they did. After settling in, my second-in-command and I inspected our route across the Rhine for next morning. A good pontoon bridge — named Hodge's Bridge after the First Army Commanding General — had just been completed, so we would have an easy run to the *autobahn* on the other side. We recrossed the Rhine on a smaller bridge carrying the petrol pipeline. Trouble was experienced with these pontoon bridges on account of the mines floated downstream to destroy them. Riflemen were posted on them with orders to fire at every floating object, and there was a constant fusillade directed at odd bits of wood and debris.

We also saw the hotel on the west bank where Chamberlain stayed during the last conference of the Munich crisis. It was small and unimportant down on the river bank. Opposite on the east bank, crowning a commanding height, was the luxurious hotel from which Hitler dictated his terms.

April 10th   **Bad Godesberg to Marburg**   **Tuesday**
This was an interesting run with signs everywhere of the magnificent engineering which had made so rapid an advance possible. The *autobahn* on the east side of the Rhine down which we travelled to Limburg, was the usual magnificent double-tracked affair striding across all other roads and over valleys on bridges. Every bridge had been destroyed and every one had been temporarily replaced or bypassed. Round one long, broken viaduct a passable track had been improvised for several miles — an enormous job in the few days available.

We left the *autobahn* at Limburg and halted just south of Marburg to refuel. A Russian displaced persons' camp by the side of the road provided tea and Indian Army soldiers, taken in North Africa, came up and greeted us as the first British they had seen.

At First Army headquarters at Marburg, Colonel Stirling had first been told that he had been expected days ago and then had great difficulty in finding out what the Americans wanted us to do. Four detachments were wanted at once and one of them would have to be made up of specialist or 'increment' officers. Whilst the consequent arrangements were being planned, we had a good meal in the American officers' mess and then went to the filthy hotel allotted to us as a billet. By candle-light we wrote out the final orders and then held a conference. All detachments except one were to be torn from us next morning, and also the detachment of 'increment' officers which we were not to see again for a long time. The commander, the remaining 'increment' officers and one detachment were to leave next morning for Siegen (the most southerly town in our allotted area), and there report to the US Eighteenth Airborne Corps. This division of forces involved much detailed work in allotting the O.R.s, lorries, stores and motor cycles fairly, but luckily everyone seemed too tired to argue about how it was done.

April 11th   **Marburg to Olpe**   **Wednesday**
When we had asked First Army about our route they had pointed to their tactical map which showed a dotted red line between Marburg and Siegen, representing where the front line might be. But they thought it was by then further on and that probably we should get through without trouble. Actually we did, but proceeded with some caution along the twisting forest roads. They were marked every now and then with signs of recent battle and had been blocked round every corner with a stout barrier of pine logs or with felled trees.

Siegen was very badly damaged and a considerable battle had taken place there which had been decisive in the breakthrough to the north. The Eighteenth Airborne Corps' headquarters had just moved on to Olpe, but we found the Military Government branch still packing. We halted the convoy, now quite small, by a wood near their billet and were warned to look out for snipers as several people had been shot there recently. We were uncertain of the proper military action to take, short of leading an expedition of cooks and drivers into the forest, so decided to risk it and do nothing.

Our orders were for one detachment (917) to take over Siegen, for two officers to go and help in the displaced persons' camp in army barracks on the hill above (18,000 foreign workers had already collected there), and for the remainder to form two detachments, one for Ferndorf and one for Olpe, both of which had just been captured.

Again we had to re-sort ourselves, but this time over a K-ration lunch by the side of the roadside in bright sunshine. Five of our remaining officers were lieutenant-colonels, so some had to be placed under command of others. There was no trouble over that, but quite an ugly scene took place when it came to severing one such officer from his car and making him share with another.

Of the two new detachments a lieutenant-colonel, Royal Signals, commanded one and I took the other. Colonel Stirling and our US liaison officer attached themselves to my party. They were both practically out of a job.

We set off for the last time in convoy, leaving the Siegen detachment behind us. At Ferndorf one detachment left us, though the map was so ill-spelt that we were in doubt whether it was taking over the right place. We went on another ten miles and entered Olpe.

I drove to the *rathaus* (town hall) and found an American captain on the verge of a nervous breakdown, trying to cope with a long queue of people of every nationality. He greeted my arrival with obvious relief, turned away the queue with *"Morgen Früh"* ("Tomorrow morning, early") and ordered the *burgomeister* to produce a bottle of schnapps. He told me he was the Military Government officer attached to one of the US forward battalions, and that Olpe was the twenty-seventh town he had tried to organise. *"Morgen Früh"* was the best thing to say to everyone. He couldn't bear it any longer and was trying to get leave, and he certainly looked as if he needed it. He exhibited the *burgomeister* — an unpleasant-looking, thickset German — suggested the Hotel zum Schwanen for our mess and billets, and jumped into a jeep and disappeared.

It was too late in the day to start being a military governor, so I went over to the hotel and helped to settle in. It was comfortable, but there was no electric light as yet and only spasmodic water.

April 12th   **Olpe**   **Thursday**
Olpe is a small town lying in pleasant forest country dotted with villages of black and white half-timbered cottages; each with an inscription or text carved on the main beam. It is the chief place of *Kreis* (district) Olpe which includes about half a dozen places of reasonable size. The population of Olpe town is normally eight thousand, but it was now swollen by the addition of German refugees from Cologne, wounded soldiers and foreign workers, to about twelve thousand. Down by the railway station, the town had been heavily bombed and five hundred people had been killed there in one night. But otherwise it was in reasonably good repair. Important roads passed through and military traffic streamed from the south whilst, in endless numbers, displaced persons came in from the north. They were said to have been intentionally driven out of the Ruhr area by the Germans to impede the advance, but the system of establishing collecting points kept down numbers actually on the road to a reasonable quantity.

We arranged detachment duties. Our Law and Order officer was to be in charge of the police and responsible for public order, another was to look after the displaced persons and I did food, public utilities, health and anything else that turned up. Colonel Stirling lent a hand whenever he could.

I went to the *rathaus* to have my first interview with the *burgomeister* and found him being arrested by a C.I.C. (Counter-Intelligence Corps) sergeant. That was the last I saw of him, much to my relief because he looked as if he would give trouble. I then appointed the deputy *burgomeister*, Herr Muller, as acting *burgomeister*, took over the *burgomeister's* office and started work.

The queue of people had to be disposed of so I handed all Germans over to the *burgomeister*, to be dealt with by him, and all other nationalities to my interpreter, Sergeant Smith. He could neither speak nor understand German very well, and, having no other language but English, was qualified to discourage any queue of Russians, Poles, Belgians and Yugo-Slavs before very long.

Passes were the next trouble. Everyone seemed to want a pass of some sort — the fire brigade to be out after curfew in case of a fire, someone a pass to visit a dying parent, the milkman one with which to collect milk from the surrounding farms, and so on. I made the *burgomeister* responsible for preparing and producing these at a set hour each day, but being an unofficial detachment we possessed no rubber stamp — the absence of which means a pass is not valid. A signature had to do instead. In practice it made little difference as the troops, most of whom had not even heard of Military Government, took no notice of them anyway.

Several German interpreters speaking good English were available, including a Dr Spies, a refugee from Cologne, who before the war had been an advertising agent for German firms in England. With their help I pieced together the situation from the German angle and checked it with Colonel Stirling who was active outside.

There was one week's bread and ten days' meat supply in the town and without transport no more could be brought in. The railway was of course badly damaged and out of action. Hospitals full of German wounded required large food supplies. Hungry displaced persons were streaming in and were being collected at three points on roads leading into the town — a brickyard, a factory and a field in the village of Drolshagen. Water and electric light plants were being repaired and it was hoped that both would be ready in a day or two. Drains were working and beyond a few cases of scarlet fever there were no epidemics. A force of temporary police wearing white *Militar-Regierung Polizei* arm bands was in action during the day up to curfew time; the action consisting of standing about at the entrance to the *rathaus*.

Clearing the streets had started, though the essential main roads had already been made passable by army bulldozers. Unrest in the town was confined to the nightly looting of food and clothes from the citizens by displaced persons. The German population was ready enough to do what it was told, though still dazed and rather inactive as the result of the bombing. We had no trouble with them and threats over the German wireless that anyone accepting office under Military Government would be promptly dealt with by the Wehrwolves and German Freedom Movement, were not taken seriously. Most of the Nazi officials had fled and the remainder were lying low.

The problem of the displaced persons seemed the most pressing and we were able to persuade the army to let us have some transport and so moved 1,200 during the day to the camp at Siegen, leaving as we thought only 500 for the next day. But by then, as many more again had come in. We pointed out to the *burgomeister* that, if he did not send food down to the collecting points at once, there would be serious rioting and looting that night. He did. There was also some looting, but it served to encourage him to better efforts the next day.

In the evening we called on the US corps' headquarters and found them very helpful and rejoicing in electric light from a generator which they took about with them. Lieutenant-Colonel Kane, who was their chief Military Government staff officer, was the most efficient and likeable American officer we met. They gave us some copies of proclamations and a *Handbook of Military Government*, but unfortunately no rubber stamp.

April 13th   **Olpe**   **Friday**
This day was a busy one with an endless succession of people and events to be dealt with or put on one side. By the evening there was such an accumulation of urgent outstanding matters that it was impossible to cope with them and it was best to leave them all and go to dinner.

First we heard that Roosevelt was dead, so hoisted our Union Jack and Stars and Stripes at half-mast. We should also have flown the French and Russian flags, but these were not obtainable.

We opened a savings bank and sealed the vaults of the local branch of the Reichsbank. The upper part had gone. We put some German transport on the road, including a sixty-four-seater bus and moved 6 to 700 displaced persons to Siegen. I interviewed the chief German Army doctor, Eric Junkers, and found that we had three large hospitals with over a thousand German wounded, some RAF and Russians. All were short of food and medical supplies and grossly overcrowded. One of our officers visited the RAF and sent letters home to their families. They had been reasonably well treated and were soon moved to American field hospitals. But the Russian wounded had been treated little better than animals and I had them moved to the St. Martinus Hospital which was damaged but usable and could also be used for civilians. To the delight of the head woman doctor I evacuated a few German wounded from the maternity home.

Colonel Stirling went out to Wenden (where were stored the properties of the Cologne Opera-house) and Welscken-Ennest respectively and appointed *burgomeisters* and told them what to do.

Another event was the visit of a VIP (very important personage) for whom a curfew had to be imposed at midday and twenty bottles of hock provided. This was General Eisenhower, who came to lunch at corps' headquarters; but we were not invited.

During the morning most of the US troops left and we thought that we had everything nicely in hand. I made a note of the events of the afternoon, which reads as follows:

> *P.M. 13th April. Olpe.*
> Following reports received in quick succession:
> 1. Russian D.P.s looting wine stores — many dead drunk.
> 2. Italian shot up road and dying. Send help.
> 3. Russians at mountain villages threaten to burn down villages tonight. Girl with message from *burgomeister*.
> 4. Three USA dead must be buried at once.
> 5. 1,000 D.P.s at brickworks must be moved at once to avoid trouble.
> 6. Cellars full of dynamite.

As to the wine stores and Russians, our Law and Order officer went down and broke the casks. The Russians then had to lap up the stuff from the floor of the cellars and soon became discouraged. He also stopped some displaced persons who were looting a house occupied by some Dutch people. He and the RSM fired a shot or two over their heads, mentioned Stalin in an enthusiastic manner, and all was well.

The news of the threat to burn the villages was brought by a frightened girl messenger. We had no troops to send and could do nothing about it. In actual fact it didn't happen.

The US dead we buried against all the rules since they should have been sent to the Graves' Registration people miles away, but the matter was too urgent for that and we had no transport.

We put our own two three-ton lorries onto moving the displaced persons and sent about a hundred to Siegen to pacify them. They imagined that they would be sent straight home from there, and crowded the vehicles to bursting. Poor things, they must have had a rude awakening when they reached that camp. It was months before the eastern nationals left.

I felt that the news about the cellars required personal attention since they were directly below me. They were without doubt full of dynamite, explosives, arms and ammunition of all kinds brought in by well-meaning persons who had found them lying about and who had thought the *rathaus* the place for them. But someone had tried to set them off for there was the mark of fire right up to the ceiling from the dynamite. I locked the door, pocketed the key and went out, only to be told later that the cellar which had been in use as a public air raid shelter, had another entrance wide open to the street. Finally we were lucky in securing an American ordnance party to dispose of the stuff and they confirmed that some of it was in a dangerous condition. A month or two later the town hall at Attendorn nearby was completely destroyed from a similar cause, but it was established that that was accidental. An unexploded bomb had been brought in and probably put down without due care.

April 14th   **Olpe**   **Saturday**
In the morning we found that Eighteenth Corps' headquarters had gone, leaving only a message centre and telephone exchange (through which we could never get a line). I lost one officer, who had done fine work with the displaced persons, the RSM and some other ranks. They all went to make up another *ersatz* detachment to take over a place called Brilon. The costly battle of Ludenschied was being fought and Colonel Stirling paid it a visit. He had great difficulty in evading Germans trying to surrender to him.

I interviewed Dr Pruss, managing director of the Rhur Water Supply Association, whose office had been evacuated to Olpe. Our electricity and water supplies both originated at the Lister Talsperre, a dam and power plant nearby, and he was very efficient in getting both into working order. The lake had floating mines in it and we got American engineers to make them safe.

Displaced persons continued to collect. Our German transport failed to return from Siegen, so only 120 were moved. An empty US convoy, officered and driven by Negroes, actually offered us its services. Besides the displaced persons for Siegen, we loaded some thirty-five lightly wounded German soldiers for delivery to Marburg. We still wonder what happened when they got there as no arrangements had been made and the only reason for selecting that destination was that the convoy was going there. But our hospitals were so overcrowded that something had to be done. I also sent off an SOS for food and medical supplies for the army hospitals. These had to be supplied by the US Army under the Geneva Convention and had not yet turned up.

We had many reports from German informers — and there were plenty of them — of parties of Nazis and SS men in the woods, but they were evasive and though we finally got an infantry company to scour the district, nothing was found. A few US sentries were shot at night but though there was some alarm, nothing worse happened.

April 15th   **Olpe (Kierspe and Halver)**   **Sunday**
The first job of the day was to revert Herr Muller to the position of deputy *burgomeister*. He was neither trustworthy nor energetic and was mainly concerned to keep displaced persons out of his factory in the town. The *landrat* or governor for *Kreis* Olpe was an absentee and had sent word that he was too ill to come and see me, so I deposed him and ordered him to report to me as soon as possible. Dr Spies, the advertising agent and interpreter from Cologne became both *landrat* for the *kreis* and *burgomeister* for the town. He was a kindly well-meaning man, though he had little drive and spent too much time talking. But he was quite trustworthy which was worth much. In spite of Nazi threats I never saw the slightest hesitation on the part of a German in accepting office, yet there was no small risk.

I went to Kierspe where the Americans had said some guidance was needed, taking with me a German woman interpreter. She had been a teacher of English at Bonn University and was now a refugee from Cologne with her mother and her baby, living in a neighbouring village. Her husband was somewhere in the Ruhr 'pocket' with the German Army and she had touching faith that I could find him if he was taken prisoner. He turned up on the day I left Olpe as a fugitive, so I had him registered as a prisoner of war and much to her delight ordered him to house arrest with her. Whether he ever became a real prisoner I never heard. We had large numbers of German soldiers coming in and, as we had no prison cage anywhere near and no troops in the neighbourhood, we could only take their names and send them home as a temporary measure.

The *burgomeister* of Kierspe was very anxious to do the right thing and suffering as usual from the depredations of the foreign workers brought in by his countrymen. I gave him proclamations and orders to post and told him to feed the foreign workers to keep them quiet. Then I went on to Halver to see our detachment commander. He had magnificent British and US flags outside his headquarters of enormous size. Arriving without any he had ordered the *burgomeister* to provide and they had been made with tolerable accuracy overnight. He had been a Military Government officer in North Africa and got what he wanted without argument.

April 16th   **Olpe (Hunswinkel)**   **Monday**

Dr Spies produced a proclamation exhorting the citizens of Olpe to good behaviour and hard work, and I approved the translation. The population was getting no news of any kind except such propaganda as they heard from the Berlin wireless station on the few receivers left to them by the US troops, so some official statement of how they were to behave, was necessary.

PROCLAMATION
to the population of the district of
OLPE

In a very serious and decisive hour we address to the whole population the urgent warning to act according to circumstances with self-possession and ordinances.

It is necessary to undertake and carry out all the tasks and duties resulting from our serious situation; calm, well disciplined and ready for reconstruction, as only in this way we may be able to restore order longed for by all of us. Every individual, men and women, boy and girl, carry in their hands the future and fortune of our country. Begin to cure the wounds of our country with all your strength and devotion. Show in all you do or leave what love and faith our homeland had and hides.

You render the best service to your country only in strictly observing the regulations published by the Military Government and in separating and keeping away from acts and instructions of every kind contrasting these ordinances.

If you want to prevent further distress for yourselves, your wives and children, and home, keep away in spirit and action from all hostile acts against the occupation army. If people of such hostile sentiment are known to you, warn them to keep self-controlled and don't recoil from denouncing them, because this is the only way you serve best our life and future. To believe you may serve your country according to Wehrwolf proclamation is mad. Wehrwolf and actions of violence of an individual or a group means destruction of our country. Heaviest punishment will follow up lawless actions not only for the individual himself but also for all of us. Sabotage of all kinds, even the slightest case will be punished by death on the spot. Everybody may help to avoid lawless actions and prevent worse fortune. Prove unshakeable will of discipline. Toughest labour with all strength supported by the idea of team spirit will alone help us and further us.

Our confidence in the honest and self-controlled mind of the population of OLPE is great; help all of you, to preserve this confidence.

(Translation of notice issued by the Landrat of Kries Olpe)

Corps' headquarters sent us an order to take food to a concentration camp at a place called Hunswinkel where the inmates were starving and were thought to have typhus. We persuaded the Siegen displaced persons' camp to let us have some food for them, but as all they could spare were several sacks of sugar and several slabs of meat, it was not really quite suitable. However I set off with Dr Junkers, the German army doctor, and Sergeant Morley in a 15 cwt. lorry. First we went to the wrong place on the Lister Talsperre (there are two places called Hunswinkel) and then to the right one near Ludenschied. It was a small camp, surrounded by barbed wire, in the bottom of a large uninhabited valley which was in the course of being dammed as a reservoir; a dreary spot and a long way from human habitation. We were greeted by a one-armed Belgian priest who was in charge. The Gestapo guards had fled and he, with a party of German Jews and Dutchmen and women had arrived there very recently after walking from Cologne — a week's journey with practically no food. Some of his party had died on the way. In the camp there was still a number of the original occupants whose crimes had been of a minor political nature or simply that of possessing relations with Jewish blood. But one German girl of about seventeen had been a member of the German underground movement and was rightly very proud of it. Some were so thin that they had no flesh on their bones, only skin covering them. They could just walk, very slowly with a shuffling and uncertain gait. Dr Junkers did what he could but thought that some were bound to die. He expressed horror at what he saw, though how genuine that was I couldn't tell. For years he had been with the German Army on the Russian front, and told me that he had been sent back because his political views were considered unreliable. He was an intelligent man, speaking perfect English, and I had no doubt

C

about his being an efficient doctor, but I could not forget the bad treatment which the Russians had received in one of his hospitals. Like many other Germans he did not regard the eastern races as really human.

After delivering the food we left, promising to return the next day to evacuate them. There was no outward show of pleasure because most of them were past showing any feelings at all. The atmosphere was one of dull apathy and misery.

On our return to Olpe we found that rations had arrived for the Wehrmacht (army) hospitals and also an American officer to take care of them, taking them off our hands.

Six hundred more displaced persons had to be sent to Siegen, mostly in German lorries repaired and put on the road by the French. Unfortunately, but naturally, we did not get them back again, and probably some went right through to France.

April 17th   **Olpe (Hunswinkel)**   **Tuesday**

We set in motion, or thought we had, preparations for turning the agricultural school into a hospital for the inmates of the concentration camp. It was to be cleaned and equipped, by the afternoon, by some Poles who were living in it and the *burgomeister* was to see that supplies were sent up.

I set off again for Hunswinkel with Sergeant Morley and two three-ton lorries. On arrival we had to arrange ramps to enable the sick to get into them and loading was a slow business. We could only take half the total of fifty-five in one journey. On the way back we made a detour to drop one or two of them at their homes. One woman was so weak that she had to be practically carried into her house by two soldiers and the reunion with her family, who at first hardly recognised her, was pathetic. She had been away for two years.

Arriving at the agricultural school, I found to my dismay that nothing whatever had been done. The Poles had not even started work and the beds were still stacked in a downstairs room. The nurses and kitchen staff were "on the way", and the place was still filthy. With the help of Colonel Stirling we started work. First Sergeant Morley and the lorries were sent back on their own to fetch the remaining patients. Then we turned the caretaker out of his comfortable flat on the top floor and put the worst cases in there. Dr Junkers appeared and was told to produce the staff and also sheets and bedding for every patient. He demurred at the latter order and said that there were none to spare. At that I fingered my revolver and sent him off with the American hospitals' officer to get them. The Wehrmacht wounded could do without if necessary. Then Colonel Stirling and I were rude to the *burgomeister* and I took him off in person to collect bread from the bakery.

By the evening the place really looked like a hospital, with two doctors and eight nurses. The patients were all in comfortable beds with sheets, and the kitchen was in action. The bread was too new to be eaten, but most of the cases could take little more than milk.

We visited those who were least ill at dinner and found them very cheerful. We had heard a rumour that Goering was dead and they actually cheered with delight, only regretting that it was not Himmler.

We enquired about this hospital weeks later: only four died and the rest recovered. But what was to be done with them next no one knew, for the German Jews had no homes left and probably no relations. For the time being the town looked after them.

In the meantime we had received orders to move from Olpe on the next day and to report to corps' headquarters at Milspe, away to the north. We were disappointed as we were growing fond of Olpe and moreover we were told that probably no one would succeed us to carry on our work. I was doubtful whether Spies could hold his position alone, so collected the town officials in the council chamber and addressed them. I told them that we were leaving but that we should keep a watchful eye on them and that now was their chance, whatever might have been their individual political past, to show themselves trustworthy. In the outcome Spies continued in office for several months.

That evening Colonel Stirling and I visited the displaced persons' camp at Siegen into which we had poured so many hundreds from Olpe. At that time there were 18,000 of them in the camp (about three-quarters of whom were Russians), and as there was no movement out of it the number ultimately rose to 25,000. The place presented a picture of a seething mass of humanity, with concertinas playing, meals cooking on improvised fires in the open and the babel of a dozen languages.

A staff of twenty-five Dutchmen and women had just arrived, full of zeal and enthusiasm for their job. The camp commandant, an American captain, said that he had two days' food and was doubtful whether more would be forthcoming. The water supply was practically non-existent because there was no electricity to work the pumps, and although some attempt had been made to dig trench latrines this had not been a great success. DDT powder was available and each new arrival was dusted with it as a precaution against typhus. No attempt had been made at registration for lack of staff. Later a Russian liaison officer arrived and his main contribution was to encourage his fellow countrymen to plunder the Jugo-Slavs "while they had the chance".

All this week we had but little idea of what larger events were taking place. We had seen no newspapers, heard no wireless news and received no private or official mail of any kind. Our attachment to the Americans had cut us off completely. Technically we should have sent back to the nearest British field post office to tell them where we were, but that was several hundreds of miles away. Passing officers, who came in for a meal, gave us the latest rumours. We knew that the Germans in the Ruhr 'pocket' were now completely surrounded and were expected to surrender at any time. The number was estimated to be 120,000 but in fact over 300,000 finally surrendered. We were told that the Russians had entered Berlin, that Goering had been shot by Hitler and so on; all untrue.

German transport was being destroyed for lack of petrol; that was a fact for burnt out Wehrmacht vehicles were to be found all over the countryside. A landau, used by German officers in place of a car, had been taken complete with Panzer divisional signs on the doors: an example of German thoroughness even *in extremis*.

Thus our move towards the Ruhr was not unexpected.

April 18th   **Olpe to Hagen**   **Wednesday**
Next morning an American NCO arrived and announced that he was taking over the town. I gave him all the information I could and hoped he was genuine. Within a day or two he was deposed, protesting, by another detachment which was sent from Halver to take over. We came across a case of one American deserter who had sewn on sergeant's stripes and taken over a village as military governor. He had done a roaring trade in passes at so many marks each and lived in the lap of luxury until he was caught.

We now all had German private cars of our own. These had been found mostly abandoned for lack of petrol. (Also to be found, wanting batteries, clocks and luxuries attractive to displaced persons.) The colonel had a dangerously fast six-cylinder machine and I owned a steady four-seater BMW. These cars made our work much easier. Travelling quickly and comfortably helped us to be more efficient and was less exhausting. The army provided only 15 cwt. lorries. One officer spent nearly all his time nosing out abandoned cars in distant corners of the forest and our fleet at one time became embarrassingly large. Even our American liaison officer had one, but we couldn't spare him a driver and it suffered endless damage.

We left our surplus stores at Olpe and drove to Milspe where we were given orders to take over Hagen, a large town which had had important iron and steelworks. Two of us went on ahead telling the rest of the detachment to wait for us at Haspe, a suburb south of Hagen. We found Hagen itself completely ruined. The *rathaus* was the only building still partly usable and there the *ober-burgomeister*, Dr Donneweg, was trying to work in an office crowded with a mob of American soldiery, displaced persons and Germans. A Belgian "Captain of Marine" with one leg, who said he was recently out of a concentration camp, had appointed himself an unofficial Allied governor, and had also set up a bureau for the repatriation of displaced persons which was busy recording their names. He was the rough diamond type and subsequently appeared in my office leading a Polish youth, holding his jaw, whom he had caught trying to get into his car and had knocked out at a blow. He wanted an immediate trial and dire punishment. I put the Pole in prison for the night and the captain came to beg him off the next day.

There was no form of Military Government in being, so I established myself with these existing authorities and set off to find accommodation for the detachment. No house was to be found in the town sufficiently intact, and our night's lodging looked likely to be bleak. We returned to our rendezvous in Haspe, and there, right opposite our waiting convoy, were a number of good houses ideal for our purpose. We inspected them and accompanied by the chief of police, gave orders for two of them (87 and 88 Berlinestrasse, Haspe) to be evacuated within two hours. Turning people out at short notice was unpleasant but unavoidable. In this case the owner of both houses (Herr Eversbusch, whose family tree adorned most of the rooms) was the Nazi *führer* of the local industrialists and ran the brewery. Also he had another house to live in. We never met with any protest on requisitioning houses. The inhabitants always accepted the inevitable as a matter of course, although they had to leave all but personal possessions with quite a chance of never seeing their property again. All Germans had been well drilled in obedience to orders without a murmur, lest worse befall.

The Belgian captain found us good French staff and we were soon comfortably installed with offices in one house and mess in the other. A new interpreter turned up; a seedy-looking individual name Pressler, who announced in broad Cockney that he was British and produced papers to show that he had served with the Middlesex Regiment in the last war. He had a German wife and had kept his job as a clerk in the big Accumulator Works right through the war. He turned out to be one of the best interpreters we ever had.

April 19th   **Hagen**   **Thursday**

Hagen was a much worse case than Olpe. Nearly all in ruins, it had besides its own population, 10 to 20,000 displaced persons living in ruined factories, railway stations and anywhere they could find. The bulk food supplies of the town had been burnt in the air raids, so they obtained food by plundering the surrounding country. I received a letter from a certain Von Gronow, describing all this and its consequences with perfect accuracy; but with no hint of any realisation of the prime responsibility of the Germans for bringing in foreigners as slaves. His letter was as follows, with my reply attached:

TO THE HIGH MILITARY COMMANDER AT HAGEN — HASPE.

To you, who now is the owner of the responsibility before God, I give knowledge of the great distress of our population.

The foreign workmen, living in camps in the town, have been nourished badly during the last months. In the farms they have usually been nourished much better than the German inhabitants of the towns. Now it seems, as if the foreign workmen in the town were not nourished regularly. The farms therefore were visited continually by foreigners, who either conveniently ask for food or who threaten the farmer families and plunder.

For the members of cultivated nations, who are not willing to plunder there remains nothing.

The plunderers have taken arms from the German military and are as cruel as nobody here has been since centuries. They can plunder as much as they want, because the German farmers have delivered their arms trusting to legal conditions.

A help by the garrison is scarcely possible, because the telephone is destroyed and the bicycles are stolen by the plunderers. Before the garrison can be advertised, usually half an hour will be passed, because all our farms are situated quite lonely and far away from the town. And so there can be no help before plundering is finished.

The plunderers do not only take what is necessary for them. They kill animals of which they can only eat a bit, the rest is spoiling. They rob the working horses, to kill them or to ride homewards on them. They destroy the furnitures and abuse men, women and children.

In about one week there will be no cow, no horse, no sheep, no pig in all the environs of HAGEN. No cow means that all babies will starve; no working horses means that no farm work can be done.

In this situation I think it my duty to ask you for the following measures:

1. Provision of the foreigners on legal basis.
2. Protection of the farms.
   Protection of the farms I propose the following measures:
   a. Disarming of the foreigners, who do no military or police service.
   b. Distribution of arms to apt persons in the farms.
   c. Protection of the farms by armed scouting parties.
   d. Arrangement of military guard in several parts of the town.

From M. J. Blancr von Gronow
Haus Herkoten
HASPE   19 April 1945

NOTE
He has been reminded that his own people brought in the Russians as slaves.
He has been told that
a. Germans will not be armed
b. Law and order will be restored by American troops as soon as practicable.

B. N. Reckitt, Lt.-Col.

We found several French prisoner of war camps, for other ranks, also short of food. I visited one with bread supplies and found their discipline and smartness still magnificent even after five years of imprisonment. They were not on good terms with the Belgian captain or French foreign workers, because some of the latter had actually joined the Germans in a hunt for some of their fellows who had escaped. I planned to form them into an armed police force to keep order and their delight was unbounded. They started drilling at once, but an American battalion arrived and the idea had to be dropped, much to their disappointment. They were all repatriated within a fortnight.

Hagen was a county or *stadtkreis* on its own and so boasted an *ober-burgomeister,* who corresponded in rank to the *landrat* of a *landkreis* such as Olpe. Dr Donneweg was an elderly, retired solicitor and not much more than a good figure-head. I arranged for him to visit me every morning for a conference, and for the clearance of the streets and removal of derelict tanks and tramcars. Water and light were in working order and there were no epidemics. The bombing had been terrible but enormous concrete shelters, several storeys high and with roofs many feet thick had made existence in the town possible. But one such shelter had been hit on its thinner side wall and many casualties had resulted. Every house in the suburbs had an excellent cellar shelter fully equipped with beds. It was rare to find a bed upstairs. Sets of ARP equipment had been supplied free to every householder and in every way their precautions seemed to have been very good. On the other hand they had done little in the way of growing their own food supplies. The local gardens were beautifully kept but, unlike those in England, they grew only flowers. Moreover the population was still well clothed, the women wore silk stockings and amongst the books in our houses I found beautifully printed and bound editions dated 1945.

The main problem in Hagen, was as usual, that of displaced persons. I spent half a day delivering bread with Sergeant Morley and in the process trying to find the camps and assess numbers. This was made particularly difficult by the camp leaders whose estimates rocketed as soon as it was known that a bread distribution was to be made. We handed out a thousand loaves on the basis of a loaf to four people and next day Sergeant Morley did the same job on his own. The loaves were of quite good brown bread, locally baked. To make matters still more difficult we received orders to send no more displaced persons to Siegen as that camp was full. We were to concentrate all of them into "one or two big camps in the district", easier to say than to do when there were no such big camps.

A week or two later a whole suburb of Hagen was cleared of Germans and made into a camp for Russians, and this was the only possible course to take.

In the evening an American battalion arrived to maintain order and with them we laid plans for night patrols to stop the plundering of farms and sporadic fighting between Poles and Russians.

The weather remained good; a great mercy for the mass of people still on the roads and sleeping in the fields, but also an encouragement to illicit night work.

April 20th   **Hagen**   **Friday**
US Army rations arrived for the French prisoners of war and they had really good meals at last.

Our Law and Order officer was busy at the town gaol checking the prisoners. Most of them were 'in' for such crimes as listening to the BBC and making adverse remarks on the conduct of the war. None of the cases had yet been heard and most had been awaiting trial for at least six months. We released all but a few real criminals. Some had nowhere to go and remained as guests for the time being.

Between Milspe and Hagen was a railway tunnel blocked at both ends by bomb damage. A perturbed railway official came to tell us that the railway chief at Dusseldorf had loaded his entire staff, archives and a large sum of money onto a train and driven it into this tunnel to escape the Allied advance. It had now been there over a week. Could something be done about it, please, as the staff were getting hungry and the tunnel insanitary? We could only report to the Americans and we never heard the end of that story.

April 21st	Hagen	Saturday

We had now counted 5,868 displaced persons dispersed in forty-three camps, and we still continued to feed them and exhort them to keep out of mischief. Probably there were as many more again to be found and I turned the French prisoners of war onto the job of finding and recording the rest.

Our one US battalion was relieved by two battalions of the US 75 Division, and these divided the town between them. A daily conference in my office was arranged so that we might achieve some degree of co-ordination. In an excess of zeal much of our work was frequently undone by the troops. For instance we had arranged for labour to be organised to clear the streets and pavements thoroughly, and since most of the workers were living outside the town they had to come in on bicycles. The first morning the American road picquets seized every bicycle, threw them onto a heap and broke most of them. What good they thought they were doing we could never discover. Their idea of Military Government was the suppression of every form of activity and they had not realised that normal tasks must be resumed if the occupying forces were to live in any sort of comfort. In a similar way the Russian displaced persons thought that they were helping the Allied cause by wrecking the waterworks, but it was really very inconvenient for everyone.

The average American soldier or GI (General Issue) looked on us as a source of supply for loot in the form of Luger pistols, cameras and wine, and my office was frequently invaded by privates with requests for things of this kind.

Dr Donneweg issued a proclamation against looting, but could

of course only address the Germans who were the least offenders.
His proclamation was as follows:

TO THE POPULATION OF HAGEN

Germans as well as other people have availed themselves of
the opportunity during the riots in the city of Hagen on
Saturday and Sunday, when authorities were out of action for
a certain time, to plunder victuals, clothes, shoes and other
articles of general use in the shops and wholesale stores. The
difficulties in the supply of food, which have been great for
weeks, have increased, so that a regular supply of the
population is no longer possible. The supply of the
population with different victuals, especially in favour of the
children, has become impossible, although all measures were
taken to carry it on without any trouble in a just way. But the
continuation of the supply is severely disturbed too.

Clothes and shoes had just arrived last week on a larger
scale for the supply of the inhabitants who suffered total or
severe losses from the air raids of the last weeks. These
articles should be issued during the next time to those
inhabitants. Through the shameful attitude of anti-social
elements it is impossible to help these inhabitants. The attitude
of a certain part of the Hagen population, which must be
severely blamed, has added to the difficulties.

I request the persons who have plundered victuals, textiles,
shoes, and so on, to give back those articles against receipt to
the shops and stores concerned, otherwise severest measures
will be taken against the plunderers, a large number of which is
known.

At first they will be permanently excluded from all supply.
The respectable part of the population is urgently requested
to assist in these efforts and to report at once the names of the
plunderers to the competent district office, or to Ernaehrungs
and Wirtschaftsamt (town hall).

If the articles are not completely given back, it will only be
possible to supply the population with victuals, textiles and
shoes on the principle of public welfare.

April 22nd   **Hagen**   **Sunday**
We received our first letters from England, and the Germans in the
Rhur 'pocket' surrendered — all but their commander, General
Modël. He was hunted for months, especially in the Olpe district
where beds in which he had slept "the night before" became as
common as those of Queen Elizabeth in England.

The question of the 'military governor' was looming large. Technically the commander of the occupying troops was military governor of the place concerned, but he was supposed to work through us in all his dealings with the civil population. This was not fully understood and *burgomeisters* used to receive orders from numerous competing authorities. Both my local battalion commanders had told me that they were military governors of Hagen, and now their regimental commander, whose headquarters were at Ludenschied, announced that he held the position and ordered Colonel Stirling to await his visit next morning.

The Colonel had intended to reconnoitre Arnsberg, and after waiting for some time, left on his journey. Soon afterwards another colonel arrived, marched into my office, and without formality demanded to see Colonel Stirling — "Colonel Stirling has gotta be here!" I calmed him down by explaining that Colonel Stirling was responsible for the whole of South Westphalia, and not just for the Hagen area, and that no doubt he would call at Ludenschied as soon as possible.

He was the third 'military governor' of Hagen that day, and the fourth was an officer who appeared quite unexpectedly from the Ninth Army area to the north. He had left us at Lintfort. There was no doubt about his credentials as his destination always had been Hagen. So I handed over to him with pleasure, and we prepared to leave Hagen.

This was the end of 917B Military Government Detachment. It had had a fortnight of lurid life and had enjoyed itself, but the Ninth Army, who were taking over from the First, frowned heavily on such improper use of specialist officers and decreed that it must stop. We must start our proper work at Arnsberg at once.

I had a last visit from the *'homme de confiance'* of the French prisoners of war, and was given as a parting present a selection of German books from the Stalag library. Of all the nationalities we met, we placed the French first for discipline, common sense and orderliness. The Belgians and Dutch ran them close. The Italians were innocuous, but useless. The Poles looted and plundered on a properly organised military basis and the Russians just looted and plundered.

April 23rd   **Hagen to Arnsberg**   **Monday**

Colonel Stirling came back from his visit to Arnsberg on the 22nd with a tale of broken bridges. Every way he tried to enter the town he found a blown bridge (*"die brücke ist caput"*) and, as Arnsberg is almost entirely surrounded by the River Ruhr, he finally gave it up and contented himself with a visit to the US battalion headquarters in the new town on the south-east or near side of the water; Arnsberg old town lying in a bend on the north or right bank.

We led the convoy which included the detachment destined for the time being to control the affairs of *Kreis* Arnsberg, while we tackled the *regierungsbezirk* or county government. I went ahead to find accommodation and by sheer luck crossed the Ruhr by the only remaining bridge, that at Hüsten. Just before entering Arnsberg I found the road, which skirted the side of the steep hill on which stood the ruins of the old *schloss*, completely destroyed by bombs. In making a detour through the fields the car sank to the running boards in soft earth. Obliging Germans from the neighbouring houses came to help and to my great relief, since time was short, lifted the car completely clear.

I entered the town on the Soest road where bomb damage was worst. The railway viaduct, tunnel and station had been the targets and besides them a considerable surrounding district of forest and town had received innumerable hits.

In the central square of the old town I found an American platoon headquarters. The sergeant in command was most anxious to help and showed me as possible billets an old hotel occupied by nuns and German wounded, and a restaurant with no windows. They also casually mentioned a Wehrmacht officers' club at the south end of the old town in the loop of the river. This proved ideal though it was short of bedrooms. The main feature was a large dining hall with a minstrels' gallery, then divided by rows of wardrobes into three bedrooms for refugee families. The building housed six or seven such families, including one of the officer's wives who claimed special treatment because her son-in-law was an RAF officer. She proved to possess more evidences of Nazi sympathy than anyone else in the building.

I also had to find offices and a house for the *Kreis* detachment. The former were easy. There stood a big block of offices in Eichholtzstrasse, the same street as the club, belonging to the electricity company. The convoy had now arrived on the wrong side of the river, and whilst it went round by Hüsten, I tackled the latter problem. One house seemed suitable but an old woman was dying in it and we finally settled on a beautifully furnished and designed modern house which had been the property of the *präsident* of the *regierungsbezirk* — he had just departed hurriedly leaving his wife there with several more refugee families.

We next visited the *rathaus* and demanded to see the *burgomeister*. In a back room of the badly damaged building I found Herr Donapfel who said he was chief of the newly formed 'citizens' committee' which had cast the local Nazis from power. He seemed to be the chief authority in existence (though there was also a *burgomeister* in the background) so I arranged with him to clear the buildings we had chosen and find other accommodation for the refugees within four hours. I also intimated to him that we should need a supply of crockery etc. in the officers' club which we were taking over and was intrigued to see him with an assistant personally carrying a supply of such things in a basket down to our new headquarters. Later Colonel Stirling ordered a mess table which was superbly made for us by local carpenters — at the expense, of course, of the town.

I crossed the river by a footbridge into the new town (there was a tank-made ford of doubtful practicability) and called on the US battalion commander — a quiet Southerner who was to prove very co-operative — and then returned to help with moving in. To my sorrow we found that we had to evict yet more refugees from another house to make room for our other ranks.

Both water and light were 'on' though water was heated by gas which was 'off'. We acquired a staff of French POW servants with Germans to do the heavy work.

Arnsberg was a delightful old county town standing on a high, wooded promontory with the Ruhr on three sides. On the opposite slopes steep forest-covered hillsides faced us, and lush water-meadows lay between. At the north and highest end of the old town, on the neck of the promontory, lay the ruined *schloss* and a huddle of old houses still surrounded by medieval walls and towers. At the southern end, where we were to live, the houses graded themselves through eighteenth century to modern, and at the toe of the promontory was the 'Park' — a steep wooded hill on which, facing across the river, was the officers' club, or casino, as it was locally called. At the entrance to the Park was a convent and fine old church containing the tombs of the Counts of Arnsberg, long extinct. Arnsberg had been owned by the Archbishops of Cologne who had frequently visited it "to enjoy the hunting and fishing".

The new town on the other side of the river, was a modern growth and in it stood a vast new building, with over five hundred offices, housing the government of South Westphalia — this was the new *regierungs* building, as it was called.

About half the town was damaged by bombing and it had lost nearly all its glass and many of its roofs, but it was mostly habitable and was an Elysium after the utter ruin of Hagen.

April 24th   **Arnsberg**   **Tuesday**
At seven o'clock in the morning, the officers of the *Kreis*

detachment were busy cooking breakfast dressed in a variety of old garments. There was a bang on the door and two armed US soldiers walked in and ordered them outside at once. All males of military age in the town were to parade in the square for checking. The assertion that they were British officers was treated with contempt. It was only when the detachment commander himself appeared in uniform that the troops could be persuaded reluctantly to release their prey. It was a lucky escape as the wretched Germans were kept standing in the square all day, and many whose last military service was in the 1914-18 War were sent off to POW camps. The Americans were very keen on house searches and wanted us to sentence a woman heavily for harbouring her soldier brother. We released her 'for lack of evidence' after a week. They had no idea of Military Government court procedure based on proper evidence on both sides, and were angry when we refused to accept a written scrawl by a private as sufficient evidence on which to convict.

We visited the new *regierungs* building, a maze of offices, with every one looted and the papers scattered on the floor. We sealed the safe, as that according to the textbook was the thing to do. Weeks later our Finance officer went to unseal it and was told that an American officer had already done so and removed a typewriter from inside. The difficulty was that any Allied soldier could announce himself as a representative of Military Government and the Germans had no option but to obey.

As acting *präsident*, Regierungsrat von Lupke, had been summoned to see Colonel Stirling and later in the day paraded the rest of the *regierungsbezirk* officials for inspection. They were not a very impressive collection and each was presented with a *fragebogen* or questionnaire to fill in giving his previous political history. This had to be done with every official appointed or confirmed in office, and if they were later found to have 'forgotten' some Nazi connection, imprisonment resulted. Like the *präsident* himself all were paid civil servants and were appointed from above. The *'führer'* system of leaders, appointed and not elected, applied right down to the village *burgomeister*. The *landräte* were nominated by the *präsident* or *ober-präsident* and approved technically by Hitler himself.

Westphalia is part of Prussia and organised on the Prussian model. The *provinz*, with its headquarters at Münster, is headed by an *ober-präsident* responsible directly to Berlin. It is divided into three *regierungsbezirke* (Rbs), of which Arnsberg is by far the largest with twenty-three *land* and *stadtkreise*. Each Rb is governed by a *präsident* whose powers are or were extensive and might be likened to those of a British governor of a Crown Colony, ruling direct with no representative council.

Certain matters, such as tax collection, were not in his hands (taxes were paid direct to Berlin), but he was very powerful so long as he obeyed his *ober-präsident*, the dictates of Berlin and, of course, the Nazi party. Each civil official, be he *präsident, landrat* or *burgomeister*, had a corresponding Nazi official whose job it was to watch him and 'advise' him if his acts were not in accord with the policy of the Nazi party.

The life of a German civil servant, unless he was whole-heartedly 'Party', had not therefore been a happy one under Nazi rule, but these civil servants had a tradition of integrity and rigid obedience to orders which gave them a certain dignity of bearing in spite of recent history. South Westphalia was said to produce the best civil servants because of their dourness, lack of initiative, hunger for power and honesty.

Von Lüpke was the best type with a high sense of duty. But he was of the *Junker* class and could not therefore be allowed by us to continue in the post of *präsident*.

April 25th   Arnsberg (Meschede and Brilon)   Wednesday
I visited Meschede which had been badly damaged on account of its aluminium works, and Brilon with orders for the detachment commander to come to Arnsberg to start his legal work. The drive was through delightful rolling forest country dotted with villages of black and white half-timbered cottages, each gay with window-boxes of bright flowers. Every now and then one would come to a badly damaged place where a minor battle had been fought and there one would see a few German graves by the roadside with a rough cross and steel helmet on top. On the roads there were still many displaced persons, little parties of a dozen or so, perhaps with a cart or charcoal-burning lorry, travelling in the general direction of their country and flying the national flag on top of a pile of baggage.

Brilon is a pleasant little market town and I found the detachment commander installed in the *finanzamt*, dealing with the usual problems created by the looting and violence of displaced persons. He told me an amusing story. He had instructed the RSM on arrival to order from the *burgomeister* a number of direction signs to put up on the streets leading to his headquarters. The RSM drew out the lettering for the painter and wrote below, "Eleven others just the same". The next morning one was delivered correctly painted and eleven with the words "Just the same" beautifully inscribed in white letters!

We now had seven officers on our Rb detachment staff and we

were trying to collect the rest up to a total of twenty-three.

April 26th   **Arnsberg**   **Thursday**
It was time to start work on Trade and Industry, and since we had as yet no communications of any kind with the rest of our area, it was possible only to start in a small way with the Arnsberg district. The old elective Chamber of Commerce had become Nazified and the officials were appointed on the *'führer'* principle. Herr Donapfel's citizens' committee suggested Adolf Cosack, a director of cardboard and other factories in Neheim, as president of the Arnsberg *Industrie und Handelskammer* (Chamber of Commerce). His record seemed to be sufficiently non-Nazi, so I appointed him pending properly held elections. The secretary, Dr Bergmeyer, had to go because he had accepted rank in the SA (Storm Troops) in order to keep his post. Dr Breneg took his place.

The Arnsberg *Industrie und Handelskammer* covered all the eastern *kreise* of our area. Its first task was to report on all the industries employing more than fifty people. The total came to 163, which was high for so rural a district and showed the extent to which industry was dispersed throughout the country. Every village had its small factory, making perhaps electric fittings in peace-time and shell parts in wartime, and adjoining each factory was a camp for foreign workers, providing at the end of the war about seventy-five per cent of the necessary labour.

In addition to the *Industrie und Handelskammer* was the *Handwerkskammer* (handicrafts' chamber) which looked after all hand-workers such as smiths, carpenters and cobblers. This chamber ran an apprentice system, held examinations for 'masterships' and constituted 'Courts of Honour' in which cases of alleged bad workmanship were tried — an excellent scheme, reflecting the medieval guilds.

An officer had now arrived from a distant assignment to help me and beginning with the factories in the Arnsberg area we started to build up a record of all those in the R.G. This was to prove invaluable later.

April 27th   **Arnsberg**   **Friday**
On this day we heard that US and Russian troops had met on the Elbe and the end of the war was only a matter of days.

April 28th   **Arnsberg (Ruhr Industrial Area)**   **Saturday**
Colonel Stirling and I toured the Ruhr towns, visiting the detachments which had left us at Lintfort and which had been installed in their right places by the Ninth Army.

First Dortmund which was one vast ruin like Hagen, only bigger. Many buildings still stood, but they were only burnt out shells. The side streets were choked with rubbish and the population was crowded into cellars and the few undamaged houses in the outer suburbs. Drains had long been a serious problem on account of mining subsidence under the town and now it was much worse with all the sewers and pumps broken. What saved an outbreak of disease was the lack of population in the worst part — the city centre, where no habitable building remained. Water was carried in temporary pipes to a few points where long queues of women stood with buckets.

We were told that air raid damage had been well tackled until November, when the raids became so heavy that the organisation broke down. Before then debris had been rapidly cleared and it was not 'done' to discuss the extent of destruction. Air raid casualties were not mentioned and it was 'defeatist' talk to refer to the death even of a relative. Thus outwardly morale was maintained throughout most of the war.

Factories, lying mostly on the outskirts of the town were not all completely destroyed, and it was surprising how quickly a plant, which appeared a hopeless wreck, could be restarted.

Bochum was as bad as Dortmund though the huge new *rathaus*, where housed the Military Government offices, was only partly damaged.

Wanne-Eickel, just north of Bochum, was a worse wreck than any of them, for Krupp's vast synthetic petrol plant was there and now lay a mass of tangled ironwork covering many acres. Herne, only three miles away was, on the other hand, quite untouched.

The Ruhr was free from smoke probably for the first time in its industrial history. Not a coal-mine had as yet restarted. But even allowing for this it seemed to us much pleasanter and better planned than our own Black Country. The slag-heaps were planted and the pit-heads surrounded by trees. There were no slums and green belts ran between the towns. The iron and steel plants were individually much bigger than ours and the 'little man', the small industrialist, had been eliminated.

The unconditional surrender of the German armed forces to the British and French only, by Himmler, was reported.

April 29th   **Arnsberg**   **Sunday**
We had a visit from an 'observer' from 21 Army Group. He was our first British visitor and the first sign that our existence was still recognised by our own forces.

The immediate task before Colonel Stirling was to bring the

headquarters at Arnsberg into effective action; for there were no telephones and at best a dispatch-rider letter service twice a week. He had only ten detachments with which to cover twenty-three *Kreise*. Planning in England had been based on population, regardless of the fact that a country district needs as much attention and more time to administer than a town. Moreover, each set of German officials must be made responsible to some Military Government detachment.

After strong representations had been made we were allotted six US detachments hurriedly trained in a fortnight. These were excellent and we concluded that Americans under command were better than Americans in command, so far as our work was concerned. They told us that what they appreciated most were the clear orders and personal backing given them by Colonel Stirling.

April 30th   Arnsberg (Hamm, Münster, Möhne Dam)   Monday
At Münster was stationed the British 307 (P) Military Government Detachment composed of about seventy officers. Their task was to look after the government of the province. But the Americans did not appreciate their existence, and orders, instead of coming to us through them, came direct through US Army formations.

However, they did exist, so we paid them a visit and saw an officer who had been with us at Eastbourne and was now their Trade and Industry officer. He was not in a position to do or say very much.

Münster, which had been one of the most beautiful medieval German towns, was completely wrecked; only the skeletons of its beautiful old churches remaining.

On the return journey we saw Hamm — the town whose marshalling yards had received so much attention from the RAF right from the early days of the war. The station-master (the subject of some verses in *Punch*, 1941, ending "Oh Damn! I've been appointed station-master at Hamm") was much sought-after by RAF and US troops and he was photographed for souvenirs to send home.

We crossed the famous Möhne Dam, holed by Wing Commander Gibson not so long before. All the bridges across the lake had been blown and the dam itself afforded the only means of crossing. It had been completely repaired, it was said, within six weeks of the attack, but the lower lake and power-station had completely gone and a gravelly waste had taken their place. The level of the lake was low, partly as a precaution in case of further attack, and partly because it had not yet had time to fill again since the disaster. Much damage had been done down the valley by the huge quantity of water released, but perhaps not so much as had been thought at the time. The main effect was to jeopardise the water-supply for the Ruhr towns and we struggled with this problem throughout the summer. As a source of power for electricity the Möhne was not important.

The Germans said that their army had intended to destroy the dam themselves during their final retreat, but had been foiled at the last minute by the waterworks staff.

The dam was heavily defended by Anti-Aircraft Artillery; wires were stretched high above the water to discourage low flying and nets lay in the water to stop mines. We visited a heavy Anti-Aircraft site, very similar to ours in the early days of the war before we had really good equipment. The guns and instruments had been put out of action by just the same methods that we were to have used in the event of invasion of our country.

May 1945

General Events

The end of the war now came quickly. On May 1st the death of Hitler in Berlin was reported; on May 2nd we heard that all Germans and Italians in north Italy had surrendered; on May 4th that all German troops in Holland and north Italy had also surrendered; and on the 7th that the Germans as a nation had signed unconditional surrender terms. The 8th was VE (Victory in Europe) day and the war against Germany officially ended at 0001 hours on May 9th.

The German civilian attitude seemed to be one of relief that it was at last all over and that there would be no more bombing, and this relief was accentuated when the first atomic bomb was dropped on Japan. A Military Government proclamation to the Germans was issued stressing their complete military defeat. But otherwise these events made little or no difference. Our work was only just beginning and was at its most busy stage.

We celebrated VE day by a dinner for ourselves (and we now numbered twenty officers). Two bottles of champagne, our total stock, had to be divided between us.

At this time the atrocities perpetrated at Buchenwald Concentration Camp were coming to light and pictures and descriptions were posted for the Germans to see. There was curiously little reaction. The attitude seemed to be that such things were of course to be deplored (provided of course that it was all true and not just British propaganda) but that there had been nothing that they could do about it even if they had known that it was going on, which they hadn't. The argument that the nation was collectively responsible because it had put the Nazis in power, left them cold. The Nazis had been better people then and once in power the individual could do nothing to remove them. Hadn't we our concentration camps in Britain too? Later when Churchill fell

ARNSBERG. Clock Tower, former church,
showing swastika in place of cross.

from power at the general election, one German said he was sorry and supposed he would be executed.

The only event during the month which might have been of a political nature was the burning of the clock tower at Arnsberg. It stood at the entrance to the old town and besides forming the gateway was also the tower of an old Roman Catholic church. The Nazis had replaced the cross on top with a swastika and the church authorities had very rightly decided to replace that with the orthodox cross. Scaffolding had been erected and the swastika removed ready for a ceremony of reinstatement, when, the preceding evening, the spire caught fire at the top and was burnt in spite of the efforts of the fire brigade assisted by Military Government officers. Hitler *jügende* boys were suspected, as they had been seen climbing up the scaffolding, and two of them were grilled by the German police, but nothing more came to light. Plans were made later to rebuild the spire exactly as it had been before.

French Prisoners of War

In a barracks at Soest was a prison camp for French officers. This had been shelled by the Americans long after the Germans had left and the French colonel had gallantly gone out under a hail of fire to persuade them not to waste ammunition. Several French officers were killed. Colonel Stirling made early contact with them and we gave them two dinner parties. They had been moved about many times since 1940 and the Soest camp had been relatively good, but shortage of food during the last six months had been acute. They had even been deprived of reserves stored away, from Red Cross parcels. The complete breakdown of transport due to Allied bombing was the main reason. The officers had made their own secret wireless set and had regularly listened to the BBC news. It was not long before they were all flown home to Paris and they gave us two parting gifts. One was a Union Jack, a very good one, made secretly from bits and pieces of material and the first Allied flag to be flown from the camp on liberation. It was hung from the minstrels' gallery in our mess. The other gift was a selection (Colonel Stirling's) of five horses from their recently acquired stable of German army horses.

Army Affairs

US troops continued to occupy the area during the whole month. The British were chary of giving us any orders whilst we were under the Americans and the Americans were equally forbearing because the British were shortly to take over; so we were little troubled by 'higher authority'. Our nearest neighbours were the US 79 Division headquarters at Neheim — a good division and very helpful. The Ninth Army at Brunswick, to which went all our reports and urgent requests for such things as coal, was not so good and as we found out afterwards, did literally nothing about the letters and reports which we sent to them. Corps headquarters was even worse and had a bad reputation for inaction even in their own army. Until the British took over we could hold no Military Government courts because they would not get the appropriate forms and appointments signed.

Major-General Rawlins of the 49th (West Riding) Infantry Division, which was to occupy South Westphalia, stayed a night, and so did Major-General Templar who was responsible for all Military Government in 21 Army Group. Both were very pleasant guests.

Our US 'commander' left us for a destination in the far north, probably Norway, much to his disgust.

Stables

Work was started on stables at the bottom of the garden; the *burgomeister* 'providing', and a bridge was built over the mill stream to the field between it and the Ruhr where the horses were out at grass. Colonel Stirling had been an instructor at Weedon and an international show-jumper. He was very keen and knowledgeable and taught us a great deal. The German army horses we had were slowly weeded out and exchanged for others by him until we had four of five good animals. All were remarkable for their manners and had evidently been very well handled. As groom the *burgomeister* sent us Matthew Koch, a typical groom who lived for horses alone. Though he unfortunately disgraced himself on a subsequent occasion. Colonel Stirling and I used to ride every morning at seven, hacking through the forest, jumping in the field or schooling at the covered riding-school at the cavalry barracks nearby. It was now a hospital for displaced persons — chiefly Russians. This riding gave us the only exercise we had time to take and it kept us reasonably fit.

Rest Houses

Towards the end of the month four houses overlooking the Möhne lake were requisitioned as holiday resorts especially for the less fortunate detachments in the depressing ruins of the Ruhr. Two were for sergeants and other ranks and two for officers. We spent several week-ends at the 'Schnappshaus', a very comfortable modern house with a fine view of the lake and forest on the far side. It belonged to Frau Flicker whose husband had been a mining expert from the Ruhr and an ardent Nazi. He had died and her son had been killed in the Luftwaffe, but she was allowed to stay and look after the house for us. She was still a convinced Nazi and no amount of argument could persuade her otherwise.

Later, when the British came, 1 Corps took over the whole Möhne district as a recreation centre and, without a by your leave, requisitioned our houses and evicted the German occupants. After that we never went again.

South Westphalia

The *regierungsbezirke* of South Westphalia, for which we were responsible, is one of the largest in Prussia and has a population of a little over two and a half million. It is shaped like a triangle with the base at the top. The north-west corner takes in a large part of the industrial Ruhr and includes such places as Dortmund, Bochum and Hagen. To the north-east lies open agricultrual country with Hamm and its marshalling yards; Soest, once a beautiful medieval walled town with lovely old churches built of the local green stone, but now wrecked almost beyond repair; Lippstadt, a pleasant, undamaged market town; and Werl, famed amongst us for its convict prison, so well run by one of our officers that he received an illuminated address of thanks from the prisoners. Attached to the prison was a large armaments' factory which had been worked entirely by prison labour — a very sensible system.

South of Soest lies the Möhne lake and the beginning of the forest country which stretches right down to Siegen. The forests cover great rolling hills which rise to over 3,000 feet at Winterberg in Wittgenstein. Wittgenstein was a principality and its prince still lives, or would were he at large, in a fine old *schloss* at Berleberg. This is a sixteenth century building plastered yellow with the windows picked out in dull red, standing on a ridge with the slated houses of the old town clustered around. We found it still occupied by the family and even the Americans had not gained a footing inside. The present prince, as an army officer, had been implicated in the bomb attempt on Hitler's life in the previous year and had been sent home in disgrace. Nevertheless he had been put in a prisoner of war camp by the Americans. The Military Government headquarters for the *landkreis* was in the local Nazi party chief's house, built during the war in the most luxurious style.

Immediately south of the Ruhr on the west side of the district is a semi-industrial area where are many light engineering factories, in lovely hill and valley country. Places like Iserlohn, Ludenschied and Altena are similar in many ways to Grantham, Retford or Newark, but they are cleaner and have practically no old houses. The churches are nearly all modern and ugly, and even in the small villages they are comparatively uninteresting. South again the forest closes in, though along the valleys are many small factories, such as those of the ancient iron industry of Olpe. Beyond Olpe lies Siegen, an important iron and engineering centre — before the invasion. That is called the Siegerland, mainly a Protestant area, whilst the Sauerland, which includes Arnsberg, Meschede and Brilon, is mainly Catholic and consequently less dour in its characteristics.

South Westphalia is the most attractive part of the British Zone and in this we were lucky, though we suffered from a stream of visitors at week-ends who had often but very flimsy excuses for journeys so far afield.

Religion

The religious question was an important one. Catholics and Protestants (Evangelical Church) were about equally divided, though the former were much better organised. The Protestants had no organisation above local level, but that made it all the more important that the balance should be kept. The *präsident* of the *regierungsbezirk* being a Protestant, the vice-*präsident* had to be Catholic. The power in the local Catholic world was Count von Galen, Bishop of Münster, who, alone of church leaders, had openly criticized the Nazis throughout the war, yet kept his office. He was equally courageous with the Allies, for in a sermon of which wide notice was intended to be taken, he accused them of deliberately allowing the depredations of displaced persons from motives of revenge and he also denounced the principle of the collective German responsibility for the Nazi government and for its crimes. In some respects he was misinformed, the fault of Military Government, but there was some truth in certain of his arguments and he was certainly speaking with the courage of conviction. Yet he was a dangerous influence for he came from the *Junkers* class and still proclaimed his faith not only in Germany, for which no one would have blamed him, but in a greater, all-powerful Germany. The provincial Military Government detachment unfortunately dealt with him as the chief representative of the Roman Catholic Church and ignored his immediate superior, the Archbishop of Paderborn. The latter was a comparatively weak character and was found by Colonel Stirling living in one room in a school in his utterly destroyed cathedral city. He had graciously been granted by the Military Government detachment at Paderborn, which was not in our area, a permit to visit his see on a bicycle!

For ten years the Catholics had been forbidden to celebrate religious festivals and, to stress our attitude to religion, we permitted them again. But there was difficulty over Corpus Christi which entailed a public holiday and which fell on a weekday. It was felt a public holiday on a working day was somewhat out of place under the circumstances, and ordered that it be held on the following Sunday. But the Bishop of Münster proclaimed that Corpus Christi must be celebrated on the correct date. Orders on the subject reached us too late for action so South Westphalia was orthodox, but later an endless succession of weekday celebrations tended to hold up work. On the day of Corpus Christi I drove down to Olpe and Siegen. Every village in the Sauerland was gay with flowers. The streets were lined with branches stuck in the ground, the houses decked with religious banners and pathways of different coloured petals were arranged in patterns leading from the churches to wayside shrines and altars. This spontaneous outburst of traditional custom after so many years of abeyance was encouraging and seemed to be also a celebration of the passisng of the Nazis.

Trade and Industry

During the month the collection of information and the reopening of what were thought to be essential industries were continued. We had an official priority list, but new first priorities were constantly ordered to meet particular needs, as, for example, sacks for flour which were lying at Rotterdam and could not be moved without them and binder twine for the harvesters. The US Ninth Army issued an order for the removal to France of all useful machinery and material and we had stiff fights to keep essentials. Sewer pipes lying by the side of the road ready for immediate and urgent use, were taken away on tank transporters and had to be recovered. But much of the material that was taken never left the country and we salvaged it later. It was loaded into railway trucks which never left the sidings because of the difficult situation on the lines. The Americans paid for nothing and seldom bothered to leave even a requisition note. The result was that sawmills and small firms were soon at a standstill because they could pay no wages and we could arrange no loans for them for lack of written evidence of the requisitions. In any case local public money was soon exhausted and advances by the Reichsbank, on our orders, against no security, were the only palliative. Local taxes were collected but only up to forty per cent of normal, and as they had previously been sent direct to Berlin, special arrangements were made to open a provincial fund to which they were sent in Münster. But apart from that the Reichsbank had nothing behind it in the British Zone except the supply of Allied Military Government notes. The management consequently grew progessively more reluctant to finance the Allied occupation and more anxious about the situation.

The water-supply, sewers, electricity grid and railways all had to be repaired and the workmen had somehow to be paid, but in spite of the difficulties it was surprising what rapid progress was made. The grid was easily adapted to cut out damaged power-stations. Even in the devastated Ruhr reasonably good water was soon available, though there was a small outbreak of typhoid at Bochum. Hamm had its sewers broken in over four hundred places and Dortmund was even worse. The provision of housing before the winter was another urgent problem, but lack of transport for materials was at that time an insuperable difficulty. Available German lorries were all needed to bring in food (South Westphalia had never been self-supporting), and railways were only working for military purposes.

My Trade and Industry assistant left Arnsberg for Dortmund, where he started to tackle the real industrial problems on the spot. Another officer came to Arnsberg to help me, especially with mines, but was taken away in a few weeks to look after the Trade and Industry of *Regierungsbezirk* Münster. He was a mining expert and especially good in dealing with the great pyrites mine at Meggen in *Kreis* Olpe which employed over 2,000 miners. Large stocks of pyrites there were deteriorating and there was danger of spontaneous combustion which would have ruined the crops over a large area.

At Arnsberg we suffered acutely from a lack of clerks, though, later, German girls became good typists in English. Our letters often took over a week to reach detachments and we had no telephone lines to them, though we were connected to the nearest US formations. The Germans had no posts or telegraphs, so our orders to them could not be sent out through the channels to the *Kreise* authorities and had to be passed through local Military Government detachments. 'Higher Authority' had no appreciation of all this and used to call for information involving inquiries throughout the Rb within twenty-four hours.

A report on Trade and Industry in the area was drawn up, which stressed the main problems, but there could be little hope of much attention being paid to them at so early a stage.

A paragraph or two taken from my report, dated 1 June 1945, may be of interest:—

GERMAN BUSINESS ATTITUDE

German business men are everywhere anxious to re-start, even on a small scale, and repairs to factories are being carried out wherever possible. Their persistence resembles that of ants restoring a broken ant-hill.

THE INTER-DEPENDENCE OF INDUSTRY

The re-starting of industy cannot be carried out in a patchy uncoordinated manner. Coal is essential for all factories, but coal cannot be produced without a host of other industries being re-started to serve the coal mines. For example, miners need lamps, so the lamp factory has to be started. Lamps need batteries so an accumulator factory has to be re-opened. Or again, if a margarine factory operates, a carton factory also has to start. There is a snowball effect which is very difficult to foresee when making estimates for coal, power and labour.

MAIN PROBLEMS

(a) What is to be done with the big steel plants? If they are to be destroyed as the main measure for stopping future war production, then the sooner the better.

(b) What is to be done with all the small metalurgical plants? Should they re-start on peace-time products and if so will coal be made reasonably easy to obtain?

(c) If it is decided to abolish the big steel plants what is to be done with the labour? Such large numbers cannot be easily absorbed on the land.

(d) The labour for the small plants amounts to a large total and the same problem arises though to a lesser degree.

The officers in charge of other functions were at the same time meeting with similar difficulties and problems, especially on the food side where the situation rapidly became acute as stocks were exhausted.

Presidency

A new *präsident* for the *regierungsbezirk* was urgently needed because Herr von Lüphe, though co-operative and able, was old and of the *Junkers* class. Colonel Stirling appointed in his place Fritz Fries who had been *landrat* of Siegen. Under the Weimer Republic he was a Social Democrat member of the *Reichstag* and had recently spent some time in a concentration camp. He was a man of commanding personality, a great believer in democracy and a powerful orator. He did not practice democracy because, as a realist, he was convinced that it could not even be considered as a method of government at the present time, but apart from that he was an authoritarian rather than a democrat by nature. He addressed public meetings all over the district and denounced the Nazis to enthusiastic audiences. His tendency was rather to dwell on the past errors and gloomy prospects of the nation than to hold out any hope for the future, but we had to admit that since no constructive plan for Germany had yet been made known by the Allies, he had as yet very little to work on. As far as we know he was never even threatened by the remains of the Nazi party and he undoubtedly went out of his way to court a bullet from a Wehrwolf, if any in fact existed.

Fritz Fries differed from other leading Germans in that, whilst he enjoyed power over others, he had comparatively little respect for those in power over him. He tried to get into his own hands matters which were not within his province as *präsident* and which should have been controlled direct by the *ober-präsident* of the province at Münster, and he did not scruple to differ from and even disobey his immediate superior. The average German loved power over others above everything else, but he also respected power in others with an almost religious awe. Consequently orders were literally and promptly obeyed and for that very reason had to be very carefully drawn up. A general instruction indicating a policy to be followed, was useless and resulted in no action being taken at all. Individual initiative, although perhaps latent, had been impossible and its use was a forgotten art. In that lay both the strength of the average German as a tool to be used by his leaders, and his weakness as a citizen. It made direct Military Government easy, but that government was intended to be indirect, using the German authorities to implement policy, and due to this failing in the German mentality the introduction of the indirect method was very difficult.

June 1945

Weser Journey

Three of our 'increment' officers, who had been torn from us by the US First Army, were still doing detachment work at Hann-Munden, on the Weser just north of Cassel. They were very urgently needed so we went off to recover them. The drive took us due east through Brilon and Warburg into open country of wide, sweeping plains dotted with a few isolated conical hills each crowned with the ruins of an old castle. At Hann-Munden the bridge was down, but we were able to cross on foot and find the detachment. We confirmed that they were really returning and agreed to add certain of their camp followers to our strength. Amongst them was a Polish artist, Gregor Sajcowicz, who had been a guerilla fighter at the beginning of the war in Warsaw and had arrived at Hann-Munden by way of labour gangs and concentration camps. He had also rediscovered his wife and daughter. He had painted the portraits of the detachment and subsequently painted every one of the officers at Arnsberg, which took him a long time but kept him in cigarettes — the only form of payment he liked to accept.

From Hann-Munden we travelled north down the lovely valley of the Weser almost to Hameln (Hamelin). The roads were good and, because the Germans had practically given in by the time the fighting had moved so far east, there was no war damage. Just south of Hameln we branched off to Bad Pyrmont, a pleasant little spa. I called on the English mother of a friend of my sister. She had married a German Quaker, who had just returned from a concentration camp and was recuperating in bed. Throughout the war she had lived at Bad Pyrmont and had suffered nothing worse than the cold shoulders of her friends. Twice a day she had listened to the BBC news without interference. She showed us the Quaker meeting-house which had been used as a Nazi party building, and she told us how she had kept her husband alive in the concentration camp by sending him half her meagre rations. Now she was starting classes in English for her German friends and they were proving eager and promising pupils.

We came back through ruined Paderborn and covered in all 400 kilometres.

Army Affairs
On June 12th, the British took over Westphalia from the Americans. The 1st British Corps established itself in the vast barracks at Iserlohn and 49 (W.R.) Infantry Division went to Neheim. Their area was exactly the same as ours, which made co-operation much easier. The Americans had generally ignored the German administrative areas and under them we often had to deal with several different divisions with widely opposed policies. Though we had been promised that we could keep our US detachments for some time longer, they were promptly ordered away and we were left with wide gaps where no Military Government officers were left. Improvised teams had again to be made up from anyone who could be spared, though we had some help form volunteers from the British Field Force battalions.

The arrival of the British started all our requisitioning troubles again. They wanted a bed and bedding with sheets for every man, and complete sets of clothing for every displaced person (between 200 and 300,000 of them). The Americans had already made a similar levy for their own troops and had clothed most of the displaced persons, but their troops had taken everything with them and the displaced persons had bartered the clothing for food. The British, quite correctly, insisted that all demands should be passed to the *burgomeisters* through Military Government, but as a result we came to be looked on as a universal supply agency and were constantly having to protest against outrageous demands. Crockery for a whole battalion, a motor boat and a grand piano were amongst the things we were asked to find. The clothing was eventually collected into depots by the *regierung's präsident* on an area basis and this scheme worked quite well as it was thereby possible to avoid demands on devastated areas. But it took a month or two to persuade the army that Germany was not a source of unlimited supply. One unfortunate result was that the civil population soon had practically no wireless sets and consequently excellent broadcasts by Montgomery failed to get across.

On June 20th, the first 'Green Lizards' arrived. They were civilian specialists drawn from British industry, dressed in battledress with a green badge and paid £800 a year upwards. The salary caused some caustic comment amongst army officers. The first batch were housed for a night or two at Haus Feuchter at Hunnigen near Neheim — an old *schloss* with enormously thick walls and an array of family ancestors painted to a standard type; not individual portraits. With other refugees, the sister of von Papen was living in the house. When I went there I was told by the army officer in charge of the party that a few individuals intended to 'requisition' the household linen, though the majority condemned the proposal which we had expressly forbidden. I gave orders that the matter was to be settled unofficially if possible. The next day the officer locked all the 'Green Lizards' into the dining-room, telling them that he would release them when he received an assurance that everything in the house would be left untouched. There were sounds of a scuffle and the assurance quickly followed.

The 'Green Lizards' were distributed around the detachments, as far as possible in areas where industries of which they had special knowledge were situated — though we had not got all the right industries for them since they were sent without much attention to our needs.

Coal
The problem of coal began to loom large. Ruhr production was barely ten per cent of normal and heavy demands were being made by Holland, Belgium and France. Our factories were running out of supplies and it was hard to get enough coal even for the power-stations. High authority would stop all internal deliveries of coal and then hastily amend the decision when the electric light failed in their offices. Transport was the main difficulty. The use of railways was forbidden for the internal movement of coal and road haulage was utterly inadequate. Elaborate returns of requirements were called for before any allocations could be made and had to pass from us to corps, corps to army, thence to army group, army group to SHAEF and SHAEF to Ruhr Coal Control. Allocations were supposed to come back along the same impossibly slow route. Our figures for June supplies were never sent on by Ninth US Army with the result that we had no official allocation for that month. Absurd orders were given, such as one to move 1,000 tons a day by road in non-existent German lorries to supply a power-station. Coal became our biggest problem and its distribution a fearful example of muddled thinking and lack of co-ordination.

The Birzlager Case
Summary courts run by detachment officers had started to function, and a first intermediate court for more serious cases was

held at Arnsberg. The judges were our legal officers, and a colonel on 'circuit' for the purpose. The prosecution was conducted by an army officer who was also a barrister and the defence by German barristers. The latter were hopelessly at sea over procedure and had constantly to have their rights explained to them and even to be told how to cross-examine a witness. The trial was conducted with scrupulous fairness with even a bias towards the accused. I attended to hear parts of one hearing. Max and Benedict von Birzlager were local aristocrats living in a *schloss* near Neheim. They were somewhat weakly-looking inbred specimens and for some reason neither of them had been in the German Army even though they were about thirty and twenty-one years of age respectively. They were charged with concealing arms — a capital offence. The *schloss* had been decorated with antique weapons from crossbow to blunderbuss, all of which formed court 'exhibits'. When the Americans came the brothers asked if these need be handed in under the 'arms' order and stated that they were given permission to keep them, which sounded likely enough. When our Military Government police officer 'acting on information supplied' visited the *schloss*, he found in the gunroom a modern rifle, a loaded revolver and some shot-guns. The defence was that these had been included in the 'American' permission, but it came out later that the revolver had been found in the woods by Benedict after the date of their visit.

The sentence was five years' imprisonment for both with suspension after six months and a fine of 20,000 Reichmarks (£500 = 1,000). We had no doubt that there had been no evil intention against the occupying troops; probably the brothers had thought it wise to keep some defence against roving bands of Russians and Poles; but it was most necessary for us to be rigid in enforcing the arms' laws. After the sentence, influence was brought to bear on us through German officials such as the *regierung's präsident* to reduce the sentence, or at least let the brothers out every month to see to their estates. The aristocracy still seemed to have great standing and prestige in spite of ten years of Nazi rule.

Detachment Affairs
We were somewhat troubled by the activities of Italian D.P.s who lived in a camp on the opposite side of the Ruhr, opposite our mess. They liked to supplement their rations with fish from the river but would use unorthodox methods of catching them. By taking wires from the overhead power cables into either side of the water they were able to kill large numbers of fish and also incidentally disrupt the electric light supply. One day an over-eager Italian leapt into

the water to collect the fish too soon and shared their fate. After that we were troubled no more.

Forests and Deer

In the evenings we used sometimes to drive into the forest and watch the roe deer coming out to feed in the water-meadows in the valleys. They were shy and when they saw us would retire to the shelter of the trees and bark their annoyance to each other. We shot several and frequently added venison to our diet. We never saw red deer, but they existed in the district as also did the rare Mouflon wild sheep. The German system of game control and forestry was most elaborate and well ordered. All forests, whether state or private, were supervised by a *forestmeister*. He was highly trained and his profession was regarded as being almost on a level with that of an army officer. Game laws were rigidly enforced and shooting most carefully controlled. Every head had to be preserved as a basis for statistics and the numbers of deer in each forest were kept to a pre-arranged figure. Hunting, by which the German means shooting, was studied as an art much more than is commonly the practice in England and the forests themselves were beautifully kept. Thinning rather than wholesale cutting was the practice and replanting was left to nature, natural seedlings being allowed to replace cut trees. That this method works is shown by the result after centuries of forest management on these lines. Not all the woods were conifers by any means. There was much beech and oak as well. The forest supplied sawmills and furniture factories and, down in Wittgenstein, a peasant industry of wooden bowls, plates, spoons and forks. There was one factory making an invalid food called 'Alphalint' from beech wood which was highly rated by the Germans, though their claims were not supported by our doctors.

Trade and Industry

At the end of June it became necessary to give guidance to the German trade organisations as to the lines to be followed in the reopening of industries. The following directive was the outcome of much deliberation:—

Subject: INDUSTRIAL   File: T&I/1

To: Industrie und Handlelskammer, ARNSBERG.
From: 917 (Rb) Mil Gov Det.

1.   After a discussion on the reopening of industry with your President, Hern Cosack, I am of the

opinion that a statement on industrial conditions and prospects is necessary. Copies of this letter should be sent to all Chambers in Rb ARNSBERG.

PRESENT ORDERS

2.	Under present orders industries may only be reopened for Allied Military needs and to produce such essential goods as are required to prevent starvation and disease among the civil population. Other industries can only open if their requirements of coal, power, raw materials and labour do not effect the production of essential goods.

3.	Permits to reopen do not constitute a guarantee of coal supply etc: they allow a firm to prepare itself to open. It can restart only if essential supplies are available for that particular industry at that time.

NEEDS OF INDUSTRY

4.	The first essential for industry is transport. The railway system is not available for regular civil supply and is unlikely to be made available for some time to come.

5.	Road transport must be used primarily for the movement of food supplies. Unless this is done starvation will result because the bulk of food for Rb ARNSBERG comes from outside the district. More and more road transport may have to be taken for this purpose and industry will have to supply it.

6.	The second essential is coal, on which depends electric power because that has to be produced from coal. A very large proportion of the coal produced in the Ruhr is to be sent to the countries devastated by the Germans, and the barest minimum will be allowed for industrial and civilian use.

7.	Industries reopening now, therefore, may well have to shut down again when their present stocks of coal and raw material are used up.

POLICY TO BE FOLLOWED

8.	It is essential for Chambers of Commerce to bear these points in mind and to act on the following lines:

(a) Advise Military Government against the opening of factories if they are not producing for Military or essential civilian needs.

(b) Advise the closing of factories wherever duplication is taking place. That is if two factories are producing the same goods and cannot work to full capacity, one must be closed and the other produce fully. This is especially important in order to keep prices down to an economical level.

(c) Prevent and discourage private enterprise from trying to start producing non-essentials.

(d) Concentrate available labour in the few necessary factories producing essential goods.

(e) In country districts surplus labour should be made available for agricultural work through the *Arbeitsamt*.

9.   To sum up, the position of Germany does not allow for consideration of private enterprise, profits and non-essential goods. Whatever may appear to be the position at present, in the middle of summer, and before Allied requirements of coal for export have been put fully into force, that position next winter will be desperate unless all resources are concentrated *now* on the necessities of life and health.

10.   This policy must be carried out by all Chambers of Commerce.

ARNSBERG, EXT. 39   *B. N. Reckitt,*
27 June, 45   Lt. Col.
BNR/RB   917 (Rb) Mil Gov Det.

Copy to: All Dets
          307 (P) Mil Gov Det. (2 copies)
          The Regierungs-Praesident, ARNSBERG
          File

July 1945

'Barleycorn' etc.
For some weeks past German prisoners of war, released by the Americans, had been trickling back. The US method was to allow those considered to be innocuous to find their own way home and numbers of them could be seen at any time trudging along the roads. Now the British decided to start large-scale releases, partly because of the difficulty of feeding the vast numbers in the prison cages and partly to provide labour for the harvest. The scheme was called 'Barleycorn' and was thoroughly well organised. Each day several hundreds arrived in Arnsberg in army lorries. They spent the night in camp and were sent on to their home *kreise* the next day. There they were registered by the German authorities and were sent to their home farms, or if they had none were allotted to a farm needing labour. The scheme worked very well and altogether about 300,000 were released under it in the British zone. A more haphazard release called 'Coal Scuttle', for coal miners, was also started under the auspices of the Ruhr Coal Control, but it was ill-organised and the lorries often arrived at the dispersal camp half empty because the prisoners had jumped off on the way if their homes were near. So no one knew how many really came back to the mines.

The Russian displaced persons at last started to leave. Trains from Paderborn took a thousand a day — a slow rate which would mean six months to clear them. The Dutch, Belgians and French had already gone, leaving, besides the Russians, only the Italians and Poles. The latter were the chief problem. They were not to be sent back to Poland if they didn't want to go, but as no one knew what was happening there it was impossible to advise them and in any case there was no way of getting them back. They were, moreover, the worst marauders and had no contact with any Polish government. The Russians had commissars sent from home who

69

drilled them and instilled soviet principles. But the Poles were virtually stateless and it seemed probable that many would remain in Germany for good.

Politics

Sir William Strang of the Foreign Office, now Montgomery's political adviser, paid us a visit to find out what was really happening. He had only just been appointed and impressed on us that our urgency for decisions on innumerable problems was quite premature because hardly any major political decisions on the running of Germany had yet been taken. The task of governing Germany with no indigenous central government in being had never been tackled in the planning stage because it had always been assumed that the main ministries in Berlin would still be in existence and that their machinery would be used. He was very charming and informative and left an excellent impression.

Non-fraternisation was abolished on 14th July, though entertaining Germans or visiting their houses was still forbidden. But we could now shake hands with them if we wanted to and that was about the only difference it made. For the troops it meant that they could walk publicly instead of furtively with German girls and at home in England it meant that their wives strongly suspected them of doing so.

An internal German civilian postal service was restarted using Military Government stamps. All the old ones bearing Hitler's head or a swastika were burnt. In our efforts to administer the country through German officials this was a great step forward for they could at last write to each other and pass on instructions.

Coal

We paid two visits to the head of the North German Coal Control, to try and resolve the confusion over coal supplies and to work out a joint plan for dealing with the mines in our area. He was responsible for coal production, but labour, mine supplies from other factories and legal questions were within our province. Amongst other things we agreed on a plan of de-Nazification. In a mine at Wanne-Eickel a strike had taken place as a protest against the continuance of Nazis amongst the management. On investigation we had found the complaint fully justified and the miners had returned to work after a purge. We planned to stop this sort of thing happening again by a general review of mine managements.

The headquarters of the North German Coal Control was in the Krupps' family palace — the Villa Hugel — a vast house standing high above the Ruhr just south of Essen. It was about the size of Buckingham Palace and had been built out of the Krupps' profits from the Franco-Prussian War of 1870, and enlarged after the 1914-18 War. Doubtless it would have received further additions now had the 1939-45 War been won by the Germans. A book was found in Krupps' private office in the house demonstrating how periodical wars benefited the Krupps' business. The regular alternation of war and peace paid them best for it gave them scope for armaments, agricultural and industrial machinery in a nice proportion. The argument was set out in as cold-blooded and remorseless a manner as could be imagined; not even omitting to point out the profits to be made from the supply of artificial limbs to the wounded.

The house had been run with a staff of 300 in, and 400 outside. Only a few of this small army remained and they were kept to look after the silver and what was left of the wines. The Americans, who had been the first in, had looted almost everything and had done much senseless destruction, but there was still some good burgundy left which we had for lunch.

The entrance-hall was an enormous room lined with family portraits from the fine looking founder of the business to his increasingly less prepossessing descendants. Opposite hung paintings of the successive kaisers, their masters and accomplices. The fittings and furniture throughout the house were heavy, ornate and expensive. Everything was there that money could buy from a magnificent library to an organ which could be played pianola fashion, for the delectation of guests. The house had been erected over an old worked out coal-mine in which had been built a swimming bath and, of course, the air raid shelters. The garden on the south side was surrounded with very high lattice screens which kept out every breath of wind and, when we were there, made it a perfect sun-bath.

The younger Krupp had been found by the Americans hard at work at his desk surrounded by telephones connecting him with his ruined factories, and he was led away to imprisonment with expressions of mild surprise, but no alarm.

Promises of better coal supplies never materialized, but later by a personal visit to a personal friend of Colonel Stirling who was in charge of all transport in 1 Corps area, I was able to get some deliveries by rail — a move much resented by the Military Government staff there through whom I should have worked.

Elections
The elections in England were now taking place. However we had

received no ballot-papers and all Military Government staff in our area were virtually disenfranchised, unless individuals had remembered to arrange a proxy vote. Only field force formations whose whereabouts was well known received the ballot-papers in time. The army as a whole took the attitude that, however well Churchill and the Conservatives had done during the war, they were in fact the representatives of policies which had ruled for so many years before war broke out. Both officers and men wanted to go back to an England with a fresh policy and a brighter hope for the future, so the bulk of them favoured giving the Socialists their chance. Particularly were they nervous of the self-interested influence of 'big business' which, it seemed to them, had too great a share in the councils of the Tories. On the other hand I heard of a whole battalion, engaged in guarding a Russian displaced persons camp, which decided to vote Conservative *en bloc* because they were so disgusted at the behaviour of their charges.

We heard the election results on 26 July, and, having expected either one party or the other to get in with a small and indecisive majority, were astonished at the sweeping Socialist victory. Churchill was felt to have lessened his reputation by indulging in ordinary party recrimination instead of rising above pre-war politics and taking the more dignified attitude of an elder statesman.

Trade and Industry
Returns of production from reopened factories now began to come in. One cement firm reported: "Goods produced in consequence of failing of coal, explosives and labourers . . . nil tons"; and this was fairly typical of general results.

I found the German branch of the Nugget Polish Company, whose Cologne factory had been destroyed but whose existence, through the efforts of Herr Deuster the manager, had been continued throughout the war, evacuated to an hospitable corner of the soap factory of J. Sauerwald at Nuttlar in *Kreis* Brilon. Deuster still had stocks of tins and some raw materials and I was able to put him in touch with NAAFI for supplies to the army. But I had to be careful to show no special favour because as an army officer I must on no account use my position to further private affairs. (I was nominally still a director of Reckitt and Colman, of which 'Nugget' formed a part.)

At Ledringsen, near Menden, I visited an embryo underground benzine factory with a Canadian who was now helping me. Long tunnels dug into the face of a limestone quarry were to house the plant, and great numbers of foreign workers had been toiling for six months to complete the work. Many of these underground factories had been completed elsewhere and they were quite invulnerable to anything but gas attack. In another year much of German industry would have been impregnable.

We had several detachment commanders' conferences at Arnsberg and each was larger than the last. From an acute dearth of detachments we were rapidly changing to a superabundance. By the end of July every *Kreis* was covered and we had to double up in places like Dortmund in order to find work for everyone. This lead to the grouping of several *Kreise* together under the senior officer, in order to save us from having to deal with too many units.

De-Nazification of officials was proceeding apace, though neither our staff nor that of the Field Security Police was large enough to cope with the vast number of *fragebogens** which were accumulating. But trade and industry had not yet been purged of Nazis and there they still flourished and might flourish more. The party was more likely to creep back by that road than by any other. As a start we deposed a friend of high Nazis such as Doenitz from his position of managing director of the big Ruhrstahl armament works at Witten. But to depose was not enough because if he continued to live in the district he could still exercise a big influence. So banishment to some place 100 kilometers or more away, but within the Province, was ordered with the proviso that any return would lead to imprisonment for disobeying a Military Government order. A general industrial purge on these lines was essential and the Chambers of Commerce were ordered to *'fragebogen'* every director or manager and to send the completed forms to us with the forms showing the worst records on top. This would give us a chance of removing the worst at once and would also give us a complete record of all industrialists. Anyone found later to have falsified his form could be dealt with on that score alone. A few *'fragebogens'* had come in before I left and I was able to take action over some very tainted owners of a big aluminium works in Meschede who had long been a thorn in the flesh of the local detachment. The legal basis was simply that such people as we banished were unacceptable to Military Government, and there was no appeal against our decision — high-handed but necessary and with the merit of simplicity. As far as I know we were the pioneers of this purge.

---

* Questionnaires

Sightseeing

Most of July was very wet — the climate of the Sauerland being very like that of England — but we were able to do some week-end touring. We went to the lovely Diemal and Sorpe Talsperren — artificial lakes. The Sorpe dam had been bombed heavily at the same time as the Möhne, but, being a vast embankment of earth instead of a wall, the damage was only superficial. At Obermarsberg in *Kreis* Brilon we climbed to a lovely baroque church on top of a prominent hill and we also visited a hunting-lodge at Zuschen near Winterberg to look for deer. It was over 3,000 feet up in forest and untroubled even by marauding Russians. Another run took us through Glohe, Berge, Calle and Eversberg, all charming old half-timbered villages south of Arnsberg.

On July 17th, the pianist Pouishnoff gave a concert to the troops at Neheim and played Chopin — the first time Chopin had been heard in Germany probably for ten years, as he told us, for the Nazis had banned his music.

Horses

'Huntsman', a big chestnut horse who was an excellent hack and jumper with beautiful manners, came on July 3rd. I rode him in a 'handy horse' competition at a gymkhana run by the 49 Infantry Division at Hüsten, and would have won but for a refusal at an easy fence due to my over-confidence. 'Rheinlied', a racehorse with alleged wins to her credit came on the 20th. She may have been fast but was a sluggish ride and as mild as milk.

We had some good rides in the woods round Arnsberg. Once Colonel Stirling and I lost ourselves on a misty morning and wondered whether we should ever reach a familiar landmark. Several times we went to the "Valley of Sighs" (Seufzental) where long fields of fine turf gave a good gallop. Our groom, Koch, cared for the horses with almost childish pride, but he fell from grace at the gymkhana where he drank too much and had to be taken home in a car, semi-conscious and murmuring "Huntsman prima" which was unfortunately inaccurate.

August 1945

The Hagen Singers

At the beginning of the month the Dean of St. John's College, Oxford — Dr Moore — visited us to discuss conditions in England with the troops. He contrived a lively debate mainly on industrial and housing conditions.

Afterwards we took him to the theatre to hear the Hagen Male Voice Choir in a concert given in our honour by the *regierung's präsident*. Unfortunately we had only received very short notice and though we tried to get local troops to come there was insufficient time. Consequently the hundred singers on the stage sang to ten Military Government officers and Dr Moore in a distant gallery, and all the rest of the theatre was empty. It was a little embarrassing, but the singing was excellent and the performers had had a packed house earlier in the day when they sang to a German audience.

The Opening of the Courts

Though Military Government courts of various degrees had been sitting for some time, they had only dealt with offences against military ordinances and decrees. Consequently a great accumulation of civil cases existed and it was urgently necessary to reopen the German lower courts. This was done with much ceremony by Colonel Stirling, first at Arnsberg and then at Dortmund and other places in the Ruhr area. Last of all came Siegen and, since Colonel Stirling had by then gone on leave to England, I had to take his place. I went with the *regierung's präsident* and an interpreter in an enormous saloon car we had acquired. A guard of honour, drawn from the H.A.A. Regiment occupying Siegen, was drawn up outside the court-house and it presented arms at every opportunity. In the court room the chief judge first made a speech condemning past practices and calling on any judge not prepared to administer fair and honest justice, to resign. None did. All the judges of the district — about ten — then took the oath which was worded in that sense, and they were followed by the barristers. The judges were a most unprepossessing lot (one nervous looking one was called Jesus Christ). In Germany a judgeship is a career which starts as soon as examinations are passed. At first they sit as junior judges and gradually work up to more senior positions, but they are all civil servants, and are paid very low salaries and depend on senior civil servants for promotion and even their retention — a system fraught with danger. After the oaths, I declared the court open, the guard of honour presented arms twice in pouring rain, and we all went off to an excellent lunch at a country house. The group commander for Siegen and the neighbouring *kreise* had requisitioned a lodge in the woods high above the town, with glorious views.

Youth

The reopening of schools and handling of youth had been very badly managed. Since February all schools had been closed. The Nazi youth organisations had of course been abolished but nothing had been put in their place. The difficulty with the schools was that they had only Nazi textbooks, and though the need for rewriting them had been recognised months ago, the planning authorities had not been able to agree as to whether entirely new ones should be written or pre-Nazi ones adapted. In any case none of the latter could be found, and the former was too long a job. We urged strongly that Boy Scout leaders should be sent over from England to start a movement in place of the Hitler *Jügende*, but this was vetoed by the French on the international Boy Scout committee. (The difficulty was, I believe, overcome later.) Finally we had to have a very limited selection of school books printed locally in a hurry and it was hoped to purge the teaching staff of Nazis and open all schools by October. But much harm must have been done in the interim, for, to order the abolition of Nazi ideas without putting anything in their places, was almost worse than useless.

The Hagen Communists

At the 49 (W.R.) Infantry Division swimming sports held in a fine open air bath at Winterberg, we heard news of the first German political meeting, for meetings had just been authorised. It had been Communist and tribute had first been paid to party members who had died in concentration camps. The Nazi dictators and their methods were roundly condemned. Next it had been announcd that the Communists' Russian brothers would soon be taking over

Hagen from the British, that all industrialists must obey the Communist party and that their machinery would be smashed if they refused. Anyone acting against the Communist party would be imprisoned — presumably in a concentration camp. Lastly, Allied Military Government was not to be tolerated and the party was to work for its removal at the earliest opportunity. Luckily, one of our interpreters had been at the meeting and he had the names of the speakers and notes of what they had said. They were in prison themselves next day for incitement against Military Government.

Murder of Captain Dixon

My last official duty was to attend the funeral of Captain Dixon at Eslohe. A few days before, he had left his unit to join the Military Government detachment at Altena and on the way had met some *forestmeisters*, who had told him that some Russians were causing trouble in the woods. Rashly, but bravely, he set off to tackle them alone, but they got him first. The Russian commissars took immediate action. The murderers were caught and shot and the commandant and staff of the D.P. camp from which they came were sent back to Russia, probably to share the same fate. The funeral was held outside a little white chapel on the green hillside above Eslohe and was attended by most of Captain Dixons' old battalion and a large body of Russian officers and men, looking rather uncomfortable and understanding not a word of the service.

Departure

My demobilisation date had now been published and I was to leave on August 13th. I had already handed over my functional work when Colonel Stirling went on leave and I had to take on his job. My successor was a 'Green Lizard', a very sound steel expert from Stewart & Lloyds, who did not relish being the senior of a team of army officers. Now I had also to hand over the Rb command. After a fine farewell party on the 12th, I left in the big saloon for Münster next morning.

Demobilisation
Monday 13th August

To Münster. Collection of papers at 307 (P) Military Government Detachment and taking leave. I spent the night with No. 40 R.H.U. in a German barracks, and sent off my heavy luggage.

Tuesday 14th August

Left Münster by train at 0500 hours. We travelled very slowly along a much damaged line by way of Wesel. Over the Rhine by a somewhat uncertain temporary bridge; Gennep, where we all got out and had a wash and a meal at a transit camp; Breda, where the track was lined with Dutch people begging for cigarettes and food; Antwerp, Termonde, Ghent, Bruges, finally arriving in the dark at Ostend at 2130 hours after sixteen and a half hours in the train. We were taken to a comfortable requisitioned hotel and given a good meal.

Wednesday 15th August
We heard the news that Japan had surrendered.

Thursday 16th August
Sailed at 0930 hours in a passenger boat and reached Dover at 1300 hours. We waited in the harbour below decks for two hours because we had arrived ahead of time and the customs officials were away at lunch. The customs proved reasonable and we were taken to Shorncliffe Camp for the night. That evening I visited our old Anti-Aircraft Regimental Headquarters in Hillcrest Road, Hythe, and the 493 battery site on the marshes — now again a field without a trace of its occupation just a year before.

Friday 17th August
Handed in equipment and left in the evening for the dispersal centre — York — with about ten other officers and some troops.

Saturday 18th August
Arrived at York at 0220 hours and waited an hour at the station for transport to Fulford Barracks. After a brief sleep we were launched on the demobilisation procedure at 6 a.m. — this included filling in forms for the various government departments, selecting civilian clothing and drawing NAAFI rations for our official leave period of fifty-six days. Then we were deposited at the station and were free men again. I was home at Roos by 1530 hours.